M. Hartheimer Harcourt

DREAMS
The Language
Of The Unconscious

by Hugh Lynn Cayce
   Tom C. Clark, Ph.D.
   Shane Miller
   W. N. Petersen

A.R.E. Press, Virginia Beach, Virginia

REVISED EDITION
ISBN 87604-047-4

15th Printing, September 1986

Printed in U.S.A.

CONTENTS

Dreams: the Language of the Unconscious —
by Hugh Lynn Cayce
Introduction   3
Some Basic Concepts from the Edgar Cayce Readings
   on Dreams   10
Sources of Dream Symbols   11
Basic Types of Dreams   13
Working With Your Own Dreams   26
Conclusion   31

A Psychic Interprets His Dreams — by Tom C. Clark   33
Kinds of Dreams Studied   34
The Psychic as a Man   35
A Psychic's Theory of Sleep — the Sixth Sense   36
Three Sources of Dreams   39
The Language of Dreams   39
Psychic Parallels to Jungian Psychoanalysis   41
The Process of Getting the Interpretation   44
One Dream and its Interpretation   45
Two Other Dreams Interpreted   47
Conclusion   48

Working with Dreams as Recommended by the Edgar Cayce
Readings — by Shane Miller   50
Method of Procedure   50
Understanding One's Own Symbols   54
Exploration in Depth   60
Contacting the Overself   65

Project X Experiments — by William N. Petersen   71
(Formerly included in "Dreams, Our Judge and Jury"
now out of print.)

DREAMS
The Language
Of The Unconscious

by Hugh Lynn Cayce

In every man there exists a vast part, unfamiliar and unexplored, mostly misunderstood, a giant within, which sometimes appears in the guise of an angel, at other times as a monster. This is man's unconscious mind and his language we call dreams. There are times when this dream-language is garbled and fragmentary; at other times it is detailed and complex. On occasions the dream world pictures are obscene; again, they are beautiful beyond compare. Any man may do well to ask himself, "Am I the master of this giant, this genie? Or is he directing me? How powerful is he? Can he, for example, accept a conscious command and heal the physical body — or can he even cause it illness? Can he lie to me? Does this giant have windows of the mind out of which he can see beyond the range of normal sense perception? What is he trying to tell me when I sleep?" Perhaps in understanding his language we can answer some of these questions and thus establish communication with "this other part" of ourselves.

Let us begin our study with a typical example of an ordinary dream and its interpretation through the Edgar Cayce readings.

"I dreamed my brother and I with our wives were out on a party with BB. I fell asleep at the table. We got home very late. My brother left the car and walked home. He and I stopped to look at a bottle of milk that was marked 'undistilled milk.' " This dream was recorded by one of two brothers who had been advised by Edgar Cayce to study their dreams. It would appear to be a re-enactment of an actual event, with a few imaginary activities added. Is it possible to attribute any meaning to such unconscious mental gymnastics?

According to the Edgar Cayce readings on dreams, much helpful information about our physical bodies can come from the unconscious mind. Symbols suggesting improper diet, wrong types of exercise, previews of illnesses, or even specific suggestions for treatment may appear from time to time. A reading from Edgar Cayce on this dream explained that it was a warning to the dreamer that his body was suffering from late hours (asleep at table) and irregular diet.

The brother was pictured as being more careful in his personal disciplines. (The brother left the car and went on ahead.) Seeing the milk was a specific warning to change the milk supply. In answer to a question about this portion of the dream the reading stated, "Change from the present supply, for this shows adulterations in same." Only by knowing whether there had been a family discussion about possible impurities in the milk could we ascertain whether this particular dream involved clairvoyance — unconscious knowledge of impure milk — or simply reflected worry over some forgotten discussion of the subject. In any event we see the mind beyond consciousness concerned with and warning the dreamer about physical activities which needed correction.

Dreams of this nature, dealing with problems of the physical body, are found to belong in one of four broad types of dreams discussed and explained in more than six hundred psychic readings given by Edgar Cayce on this subject. The other three general types are dreams of: self-observation, psychic perception, and spiritual guidance. Most of the Edgar Cayce readings deal with interpretations of individual dreams. Many contain explanations of symbols and suggestions for using one's own dreams to advantage in physical, mental, emotional and spiritual affairs of everyday living.

Though the readings on dreams constitute only a small part of the total volume of readings — six hundred out of approximately fifteen thousand — they contain a variety of examples of extended activities of the unconscious mind. Students of psychology who have examined this data have been intrigued by such salient features as: comparisons with standard dream studies *developed since the Edgar Cayce readings were given;* what appear to be original insights into the interpretation of dream symbols; consideration of telepathy, clairvoyance, precognition and other psychic factors in dreams; and some interesting ideas on time-space. The Edgar Cayce data seems to suggest that dreams are an important and safe doorway to the unconscious mind, which is as available to the average person as a pencil and tablet on his bedside table.

4

Before considering examples of the other types of helpful dreams, the kind that any individual may be having daily without being aware of their meaning, let us examine some of the general statements from the readings on the range and importance of dreams.

For through these [dreams] the entity may more perfectly understand those laws which pertain to the manifestation of the psychic forces in the material world. And many of these, we see, pertain to the physical conditions . . . though the conditions are presented at times in emblematical form. . .   137-4

Another reading points out that through dreams a person:

. . . may gain the more perfect understanding and knowledge of those forces that go to make up the real existence – what it's all about and what it's good for – if the entity would but comprehend the conditions being manifested before same.   140-6

The terms "dreams" and "visions" seem to be used interchangeably, although, as will be seen, a vision may deal more with spiritual implications.

. . . the visions. . . may be used for the development of the entity in mind, body, soul, spiritually, mentally, financially.   341-12

With dreams and visions which come to the individual, these are of various classes and groups, and are the emanations from the conscious, subconscious, or superconscious, or the combination and correlation of each depending upon . . . the personal development of the individual, and are to be used . . . for the betterment of such an individual.   39-3

. . . with the dreams which come. . . These, as we see, may be used to the edification of the entity into that of how spiritual laws are manifested in the physical world.   136-14

Perhaps the term "channel" as used in the following refers to the area of the mind:

Dreams which come to a body are of a different nature and character, dependent upon the channel through which these are brought to the physical consciousness; yet often, even though of experience of the subconscious mind, they may influence an individual as to the trend or blend of the mental action of the mind for quite a period, or until something else may fill the consciousness. Consciousness, in this sense, is not wholly that known in the physical as sensuous consciousness, rather an attribute, then, under such conditions, of the subconscious than of the conscious mind.   903-5

The following extract on sleep presents a provoking thought on the basic nature of dreams.

Sleep is that period when the soul takes stock of what it has acted upon, from one rest period to another; drawing comparisons, as it were, that make for harmony, peace, joy, longsuffering, patience, brotherly love and kindness — fruits of the spirit; or hate, harsh words, unkind thoughts and oppressions which are fruits of Satan. The soul either abhors what it has passed through, or it enters into the joy of its Lord.   364-4

The second important, and perhaps the most voluminous, type of dream may be said to deal with understanding oneself. Into this broad category would fall wish-fulfillment dreams, suppressions, symbolic conflicts between the lower and better natures, unconscious work on problems, and many other familiar dream forms. Here is an example of such a dream which was presented to Edgar Cayce for interpretation. A symbol is used for another person who is affecting the dreamer's life. It must have been a rather horrible dream experience.

Q-1—Morning of May 6, 1927. I was standing in the back yard of my home — had my coat on. I felt something inside the cloth on the cuff of my left-hand coat sleeve. I worked it out, but it was fastened in the cloth and broke off as it came out, leaving part in. It proved to be a cocoon and where broken a small black spider came out. The cocoon was black and left a great number of eggs — small ones — on my coat sleeve, which I began to break and pull off. The spider grew fast and ran away, speaking plain English as it ran, but that I do not remember, except that it was saying something about its mother. The next time I saw it, it was a large black spider which I seemed to know was the same one grown up, almost as large as my fist — had a red spot on it, otherwise was a deep black. At this time it had gotten into my house and had built a web all the way across the back inside the house and was comfortably watching me. I took a broom, knocked it down and out of the house, thinking I'd killed it, but it did more talking at that time. I remember putting my foot on it and thought it was dead. The next time I saw it, it had built a long web from the ground, on the outside of the house in the back yard, near where I first got it out of my sleeve — and it was running up toward the eave fast when it saw me. I couldn't reach it but threw my straw hat in front of it and cut the web and the spider fell to the ground, talking again, and that time I hacked it to pieces with my knife.

A-1 — In this there is seen the emblematical (symbolic) conditions of those forces as are being enacted in the life of this body. And, as is seen, both the spider and the character of same are as warnings to the body as respecting the needs of the body taking a definite stand as respecting the relations of others who would in this underhanded manner take away from the body those sur-roundings of the home — that are in the manner of being taken — unless such a stand is taken. For, as is seen, the conditions are of the nature emblematically shown by the relations of this body with this other body; that its relations at first meant only the casual conditions that might be turned to an account of good, in a social and financial manner; yet, as has been seen, there has come the constant drain on the entity, not only in the pocket but in the affections of the heart, and now such threaten the very foundations of the home; and, as seen, threaten to separate the body from the home and its surroundings; and unless the entity attacks this condition, cutting same out of the mind, the body, the relations, the conditions, there will come that (threatened) condition as seen [in the dream].

Take the warning, then. Prepare self. Meet the conditions as a man, not as a weakling — and remember those duties that the body owes first to those to whom the sacred vows were given, and to whom the entity and body owes its position in every sense; as well as the duty that is obligatory to the body or those to whom the entity, the body, should act in the sense of the defender, rather than bringing through such relations those dark underhanded sayings, as are seen, as said by that one who would undermine, as well as are being said by those whom the body may feel such relations are hidden from; yet these have grown to such extent as may present a menance to the very heart and soul of the body of this entity. Beware! Beware!   2671-5

The dreamer was involved with a woman outside his marriage. Apparently, he did not heed the warning. Divorce, loss of home, children, and business followed. Here the unconscious language describes in vivid symbols the problems being faced. Self is seen in conflict and the problem is clearly defined. In the light of Freudian dream symbology some of the details, the knife for example, would bear further examination. In passing, it is interesting to note the apparently clairvoyant insight through the readings regarding the affair which was wrecking the home.

An example of the third type, the dream with a psychic content, is found in the following from the Edgar Cayce readings:

July 12, or early morning, July 13, 1925. Dreamed a man was trying to sell me a radio. Then someone put poison on the doorknob of my door and urged me to come and touch it. I was terribly frightened. He tried to force me to touch the poisoned knob. Struggling, I awakened in a cold sweat.

In this we have a presentation to this mind of conditions that are to arise in the physical affairs of the body. The presentation of a sale attempting to be made of radio refers to the deal that will be offered the individual in radio stocks or corporations, or such, offered as a wonderful proposition to the body. The presentation of poison being placed by someone on the door represents the conditions that would enter into same if the body were to accept or to invest in such conditions, corporations or stocks of that nature. Hence the warning as would come from this at the present or during this time — next sixteen to twenty days: Do not invest in stocks, bonds, or any conditions

So far as this example is concerned it is not our object to establish this as a bonafide example of precognition. To do this it would be necessary to know how much this individual knew about radio stocks, what he had read, what conversations he had entered into on the subject, etc. It would also be necessary to know whether offers involving radio stock were presented within the sixteen to twenty days following the dream. We have no access to such information. However, we have on file a letter dated July 19, 1925, which suggests accuracy. The letter in part reads as follows.

"The radio reading is surely wonderful. It was like hanging out a red lamp as a danger signal to save us from the ill effects of our own errors."

Two points are clear. The Edgar Cayce psychic reading interpreted the "radio" dream as a precognitive warning. The individual involved considered the dream as a warning.

The fourth and final of the dream classifications to be considered here comprises visions apparently containing spiritual guidance.

One of the earliest dreams for which Edgar Cayce sought an interpretation was one of his own in which he saw a close associate and himself standing in a rocky area. Running water separated groups of people whose general character was identified by their surroundings. Edgar Cayce saw a fish and attempted to catch it. The fish was broken and he attempted to put the pieces together.

On January 13, 1925, in an unconscious state, he gave the following on this dream.

This was a vision. In the dream of the water, with the separating of the acquaintances and the body, we find the manifestation again of the subconscious forces, the water representing the life, the living way, that separates those of every walk of life and (exists) about each entity or group, building that which radiates in earth's sphere or in a spiritual sphere, the deeds done in the body.

In the fish is the representation of Him who became the Living Way, the Water of Life, given for the healing of the nations; in the breaking, in the separation there will yet be brought the force that will again make this the Living Way, the perfect representation of the force necessary to give life to all.

In this condition regarding the material forces necessary for the material manifestations of the work on the earth plane there is given a way by which many groups, through two individuals, may work out that necessary for the performance of much given in visions and dreams.   294-15

Notice the universal quality of the symbols in this dream, or vision: water — life, the living way, and the fish — the Christ.

Apparently this dream concerned the goals and purposes of the individuals seen in it. The nature of the dream seems to be determined by the meaning of the symbols.

Some Basic Concepts from the Edgar Cayce
Readings on Dreams

With these examples of four general types of dreams in mind we may turn to some of the basic concepts which can be deduced in this approach.

One of the first references to dreams is found in a series of general readings on philosophical subjects. These readings were secured in several sessions early in October, 1923, by a group of men, one of whom obtained the first life reading from Edgar Cayce on October 11, 1923.

As in dream, those forces of the subconscious when taken as correlated with those (dream) forms that relate to the various phases of the individual, give to that individual a better understanding of self, when correctly interpreted, or when correctly answered.

Forget not that it has been said correctly that the Creator, the gods and the God of the Universe, speak to man through his individual self. Man approaches the more intimate conditions of that field of the inner self when the conscious (self) is at rest in sleep or slumber, at which time more of the inner forces are taken into consideration and studied by the individual (not someone else). It is each individual's job, if he will study to show himself approved (by God, his Maker) to understand his individual condition, his individual position in relation to others, his individual manifestation, through his individual receiving of messages from the higher forces themselves (thus, through dreams).

In this age – at present 1923 – there is not sufficient credence given dreams; for the best development of the human family is to give the greater increase in knowledge of the sub-conscious soul or spirit world. 3744-4

Several persons closely associated with the work being carried on in connection with Edgar Cayce at this period began to record their dreams, study them and frequently secure readings from Edgar Cayce devoted to their interpretation. Through the years these personal readings recommended that individuals study their dreams. For one person a reading gave:

Yes, we have the body here, and the dreams with their lessons as may be gained from them. In giving this we must first take into consideration the conditions surrounding the mental forces of the body through which these dreams or visions were given . . . there have been few that the body retains in their entirety . . . 106-6 [5-17-25]

For another individual who asked for help in developing his psychic abilities the reading gave:

10

. . . for the psychic forces are the projection of souls' development in the earth . . . the body should not attempt to consciously prevent the losing of self in sleep or slumber for through this we will find the first action of the psychic making the physical manifestation to the conscious mind.   137-5 [11-2-'24]

Another reading:

. . . the dreams are that, that the entity may gain the more perfect understanding and knowledge of those forces that go to make up the real existence — what it's all about and what it's good for — if the entity would but comprehend the conditions being manifested before same."   140-6 [11-7-'25]

Each introduction to the readings on dreams states in a variety of ways the importance of using this help from the unconscious level.

. . . and may be used in the way of the entities' development . . .
341-18 [1-9-'26]

The dreams which come to the body give the lessons . . . there will come the more perfect understanding . . .   538-13 [10-7-'25]

From these readings there emerges more and more emphasis on the importance of dreams as a way of understanding the remarkable area of man which has come to be known as the "unconscious." Dreams are pictured at the language of this aspect of the mind.

Sources of Dream Symbols

Apparently the mind stores away impressions received through all of the five senses — hearing, seeing, tasting, smelling, feeling. Any of these stored impressions may be used as dream symbols, in fragments or as complete scenes. Our question should be, "Is this just a flash of memory, released by some inner mechanism of association, or do the symbols have meaning? Are they a message from the giant?" A brief survey of some of the more obvious sources of these dream symbols may help us understand why we are our own best interpreters of dream patterns.

Childhood Memories. — Every childhood experience, especially those that have strong emotional impact, may become part of the dream language. The love for a dog, for example, may establish the dog as a symbol of companionship and faithfulness, or a traumatic experience with an angry dog may establish it as a symbol of danger and fear.

The Day's Activities. — Even the most cursory examinations of dreams will reveal that many of them pertain to the day's affairs. Hopes and worries regarding business or social activities may be intermingled with apparent solutions to problems. Sometimes the dreams seem to re-enact an event; at others the dream pictures the event as one would like to have had it occur. Our question should be again, "Are some of these events or actions symbols for deeper meanings, more serious concerns?" Freudian interpretations of well-known sex symbols such as pencils, knives, poles, etc. for the male sex organ — illustrate the way in which ordinary objects are used as symbols in dreams. However, it would not be wise to attribute some deep, complicated sex meaning to all dreams, any more than to every thought. It is suggested that all dreams have some meaning and that even though they may deal with daily affairs they can have more complex meaning than may at first appear.

Mental Food. — What do you read? What motion pictures and TV shows do you spend time with? These, along with daily observations, become the material out of which some of your dreams are made. What a vast storehouse, what a reservoir! What a computer our mind seems to be!

Racial memory; — universal symbology. — There seems evidence to suggest that dreams may also partake of a universal language of symbols. The unconscious seems at times to be using symbols which have common denominators, or common meaning in terms of our culture, our religions, our times. We must evidently take into account that racial heritage, through the genes and chromosomes, may play a part in the dream language, or that a division of self in time, through rebirth, may also provide additional patterns at times from the inner self. Water is generally considered as representing the deeper self, the unconscious, or, for a religiously inclined person, it is a spiritual symbol, associated, let us say, with baptism. The old man with white hair and beard is an authority figure, the higher self.

Psychic Content. — We must look also to the possibility that the mind through telepathy, clairvoyance, communication with other dimensions, precognition, and so forth, picks up material which may be brought to consciousness in dreams. Indeed, the dream world appears to be one of the safest and quickest approaches to the psychic world of man.

Religious Symbology — Our religious heritage constitutes so important a factor in our lives, especially in the early years, that we should recognize it as one of the important sources of dream symbols. The devil, the apple, the snake, the mountain, the cross — to mention only a few — have each a specific meaning for the average person if he will simply give some thought to answering, about each, the question, "What does this mean to me?"

The Body. — One of the most obvious sources of dream symbols is the human body. Parts of the body frequently appear in dreams related to their functions — the stomach associated with eating, the mouth with speaking, the hand with doing or accomplishing something, and so forth. A series of enlightening interpretations is found in the references to parts of the body in the index of 600 Edgar Cayce readings on dreams.

A lady visiting Virginia Beach for the first time was launched on a lengthy narrative when she stopped suddenly, exclaiming, "You know, I have had a very strange dream. I have had it since childhood, once or twice a year. I see myself throwing away handfuls of my teeth. As I throw one handful down I am conscious of another mouthful of loose teeth." I referred her to the reading file on dreams in our library. For one person, in two different readings, Edgar Cayce interpreted false teeth as damaging words. For this same person specific teeth referred to some needing attention. For another individual who dreamed of falling and knocking out teeth as a result of a particular friend's action a warning was given pertaining to the words of this friend which could injure the dreamer. So do our dreams use parts of the body as symbols.

A study of the Edgar Cayce data on dreams suggests a range of unconscious mental activity far more complex than we recognize in our ordinary appraisal of ourselves. Just as we have little understanding and appreciation of the marvelous complexity of the human eye and its function, so it is even more apparent that we have a very meager knowledge of our mental activity as reflected in our dreams. To put it clearly, let us ask, "Do our dreams reflect only the hodgepodge of frustrations, suppressions, and bits of important perception pushed into the deeper mind? Or is it possible for us to catch a glimpse of a higher self through the window of the mind which we call dreams?" Let us return now to the four basic types of dreams which we first cited: Physical, self revealing, psychic and spiritual dreams.

Basic Types of Dreams

Physical: October 13, 1925 — Just as I was awakening I felt myself in the same poor physical condition as last winter. I was in one of my fainting spells and Enna, our baby's nurse, seemed to be trying to revive me. Then I really did awaken.

The [dream is a] warning to the entity to carry out fully those suggestions as have been given for the entity, taking that for the system, that will bring the equalizing conditions throughout the system, for it is, as is seen, lack of metabolism in the system that causes the distresses to the body. Be warned and act. 137-22

Here there was indicated a direct warning of a bad physical condition. All physical dreams are not so easily interpreted. Apparently this person had started some type of treatment. He had recognized the trouble and was trying to do something about it. The warning was not blocked by an attitude of refusal to recognize the condition. The physical condition is visualized without symbolism.

In examining another dream which is interpreted in the Edgar Cayce readings as related to the physical body we find interesting symbols used.

May 6, 1926 — I was at what seemed to be a family party. We were eating refreshments when E.B. and someone started to fight. Hot words led to a fist fight and I finally separated them.

The interpretation in a reading included the following:

In this there is presented to the entity that warning as to the diet (influencing) the physical forces to the body . . . (represented as an individual), (another) individual representing certain conditions in the physical or moral plane . . .

The individual had been advised to take only certain types of stimulants; evidently he was indulging in other stronger stimulants. The dream warned him of the physical upset which would result, symbolized by the fighting.

The interpretation goes on to explain.

. . . there has been given that the entity should take more stimulants occasionally . . . in taking the sweets in certain forms there produces a different type of alcohol in the body itself.

Fighting symbolizes this conflict. The fighting takes place between the individual who represented the mental and moral decision and another person who represents, shall we say, the physical or lower self.

Self and aspects of self appear in many guises in our dreams. It is safe to say that a man spends more time thinking about himself than anything else. There is no reason to believe that this thinking stops in sleep. The self masquerades in a variety of forms, as will be seen.

In examining a final dream relating to the physical body we can observe the unconscious apparently solving a problem in a direct fashion. To understand the dream it is necessary to be acquainted with the circumstances surrounding it. A man and his wife on a visit to

14

Phoenix, Arizona, in the spring of 1959 heard a lecture I gave on dreams. They resolved to begin recording and studying their own. On returning to Canada where they lived this couple discussed dreams with their small study group. Members of this group were praying daily for one other. The husband of our couple had for many years been afflicted with asthma. The group was praying especially for him at this time. Here is the account of the dream as taken from the wife's letter.

" . . . After listening to your tape on 'Dreams' from the Phoenix Conference we decided to try remembering our dreams and feel that we received one message of real benefit to a member of our group. One man, Mr. X, had an asthmatic condition and would have such severe coughing spells that he would black out at times. The doctors seemed to be puzzled, said it was an unusual condition and couldn't help him much.

"At our next meeting, a week after hearing the tape, Mrs. X recalled a brief but vivid dream she had had. It didn't mean anything to her but she related it, anyway, as follows: She could see a hand come out and pour two ounces of lemon juice into a glass, then come back and add an ice cube. Just the hand. That's all there was to it yet it was very vivid in her memory. As we had been remembering Mr. X in our meditation period, we felt that it was a message, so suggested that Mrs. X give her husband two ounces of lemon juice each day and just try it. It couldn't do any harm, anyway. The results are that after two weeks' time his cough was so much better that he hasn't blacked out since (four months) and his cough or asthmatic condition is completely cleared up. The odd part of it was the fact that he enjoyed the lemon and could take it straight with just the ice in it. His system must have needed it."

At this point nothing mystical or magic is suggested. The unconscious seems to be operating at a very practical level. You may wish to assume that the wife had somewhere read of the help that lemon juice could bring to asthma. She stored this away and it simply came to the surface of consciousness in the dream state. You may also wish to believe that this was a psychosomatic condition, which responded more to the suggestion than to any specific benefits from the lemon juice. I am sure the gentleman involved will be glad to agree with either or both ideas — so long as you recognize the result — the relief from years of suffering from asthma. The unconscious apparently has the power to warn the conscious of impending physical troubles, to analyze acts which are causing difficulties and to suggest treatment. Obviously, dreams would be important to us if they related only to physical conditions. In any case we should ask ourselves, "What would have happened if this woman had not been recording and studying her dreams?"

Self-revealing. — Turning from dreams associated with the physical body we come to a broad category which is loosely related to self-knowledge. This grouping might be compared with a department store where many items are housed under one roof, or to a confederation of states described as a nation. Some of the types of dreams found in this category have already been listed: wish fulfillment, suppressed desires, worry, problem solving. Other types include an extensive group which show conflict between two areas of the mind, such as childhood religious concepts and the new scientific concepts of a college experience. Some of the most interesting dream experiences reveal the variety of I's, as George Gurdjieff, author of "All and Everything" would put it, which lie beneath the outer personality of the average person. A gorilla may represent animal nature; a mad man, the anger which sometimes sweeps over one; a ship's captain may symbolize the established principles, the higher self; a particular place, such as a house where one once lived, may relate to a traumatic experience there; a rough road may signify the difficult experiences which a person is passing through. It would not be possible to catalogue all the dreams which fall into this broad grouping, much less give examples. Perhaps the selections which follow will help us to recognize the type when dealing with our own dreams.

Here is a short one which the Edgar Cayce readings interpret in a neat fashion.

Tuesday, November 24, 1925 – In combing my hair, found in one place my hair was knotted and kinked.

This is emblematic (of a) condition of kinks in the self, as regards some specific conditions in which the entity forms too quick a conclusion, see? This, and the date, should bring to the entity's mind that condition, see? Then consider again and act well in same.

Many dreams are far more complicated and require analysis in the light of past experience and established attitudes. The picture of self which emerges is frequently far from complimentary. This is probably one of the major reasons why we do not remember our dreams. We are not willing to face the unpleasant facets of our own natures. Sigmund Freud, the father of psychoanalysis, who spoke of dreams as the royal road to the unconscious, made an outstanding contribution in revealing the depths of this lower nature.

It will be seen later that there are many symbols for the lower self, including a number of different animal forms.

One of the symbols mentioned above which reveals a negative area of self and self's actions is interpreted in the following reading:

Tuesday morning, November 3, 1925: My husband, his mother, and I were living together in a house in New Jersey. – I heard much shooting and excitement. All of the windows of our house were open and it was raining and storming outside; we rushed to close and lock them. Some terrible wild man seemed to be running through the town shooting and causing great trouble, and the police were chasing him.

Edgar Cayce from the unconscious state interpreted the dream thus:

The large man, the bugaboo, that comes to the entity in these emblematical (symbolic) conditions here presented, and as seen in others, is in self and self's temper, see? 136-18

The following is another dream of the person just quoted. This death experience symbol is interpreted in a thought-provoking manner.

[6-23-'25]: Dreamed I died.

Interpretation:

This is the manifestation of the birth of thought and mental development awakening in the individual, as mental forces and physical forces develop. This, then, is the awakening of the subconscious, as is manifested in death of physical forces, being the birth in the mental. 136-6

A helpful approach this, in explaining a dream of death, which is frequently a depressing thought.

The following dream seems to deal with a conflict between the higher self, which is attempting to help, and the lower self, which is in trouble.

[10-26-'25] Dreamed of being at home. Two people seemed to be with me. We were watching a dirigible and an air ship which were sailing above us but seemed to be in great distress. Suddenly the dirigible spun on its nose and crashed to the ground on the lawn. I heard the cries and groans of the occupants as the ship struck. The two other people and I started towards the wreck but were at first warned back by those who survived. A little later we were called on to help carry the injured ones to the house. The man I carried seemed to have hurt his leg and kept crying not to take his leg off. Later it seemed that I was again at the wreck. I drank something from a bottle and then continued to collect tools, a hammer and other things.

In this again the emblematical (symbolic) conditions of life are presented to the entity. In that of the dirigible and flying machine, those high ideals as are held in the entity's mind without sufficient stability, show that destructive

17

forces may come to such without that strength of character in the tried and true ways. The assistance as is seen is the call of self to aid self, as it were, in that way the entity would take.

The assistance and the call not to take or remove portion of body indicates that the entity sees in the self conditions that may arise, making it necessary in the life's work, see? to remove portions of same, unless kept in the straight and narrow way.

The taking from the bottle represents, then, the water or the assistance of life, presented in that straight and narrow way. The gathering, then, of tools, that necessary working paraphernalia for the successes the entity would accomplish. The lesson, then, is seen.   341-13

In considering this dream note the symbols which are used by the dreamer's unconscious; the dirigible, the high ideal, which crashes; the two aspects of self, one helping the other; the part of the body which may be lost is a portion of the life's work which must be given up unless the ideals are adhered to; and the water, as help from the spiritual influences.

That is the dream of an eighteen-year-old college boy. The dirigible falls on the lawn of the childhood home, associated with youthful dreams. The tools which were assembled could easily be associated with work done each summer on this home place during the high school and college years. Yet, it should be seen, the tools are only symbols of what is needed for success.

The following symbols and their brief interpretation from the Edgar Cayce readings should not be used like a dream book to look up the meaning of your dream symbols. They are given here to fill out the pattern of this large category dealing with understanding self. A few words of a foreign language can be confusing and inadequate. Each person should study the language of his own unconscious, realizing that even the symbols that seem most obvious are frequently used in one's own dreams in a very individual manner.

Water — Source of life, spirit, unconscious

Boat — Voyage of life

Explosion — Turmoils

Fire — Wrath, cleansing, destroying

A person — Represents what the dreamer feels toward that person

Clothing — Way one appears to others

Animals — Represent some phase of self, according to what one feels about the animal seen. In this area especially the universal, historical, and racial quality of meanings must be considered. For example, the bull, sexless human figure, lion and eagle may for many persons symbolize the four lower vital centers of the body: the sex glands, cells of leydig, adrenals, and thymus, in that order. The snake is both a wisdom symbol and a sex symbol, associated with the kundalini. When raised to the higher centers in the head it becomes the wisdom symbol.

Fish — Christ, Christian, spiritual food

Dead leaves — Body drosses

Mud, mire, tangled weeds — That needing cleansing

Naked — Open to criticism, exposed

Q — Are my dreams ever significant of spiritual awakening?

A — As is experienced by the entity, there are dreams and visions and experiences. When only dreams, these too are significant — but rather of the physical health, or physical conditions. In visions there is oft the inter-between — subconscious mind — giving expressions that make for an awakening between the mental consciousness and that which has been turned over and over in the physical consciousness being weighed with what you hold as an ideal. In visions where there are spiritual awakenings, these are seen most often in symbols or signs. In training yourself to interpret your visions, the expressions of eye, hand, mouth, posture or the like must be understood in your own language. When these are, then, (appropriately) symbolic know the awakening is at hand. 269-9

Our dreams are most surely in a great measure related to the self. Let us turn now to an examination of some examples of the mind's activity at a psychic level. Here the dream may reflect our reach to other persons and places.

Psychic Dreams. — Considerable emphasis is placed in the Edgar Cayce readings on the psychic content of our dreams. In fact, as has been mentioned, the dream state may be the safest, quickest way for most of us to become aware of the natural, but little recognized, capacities of the mind known currently as E.S.P. Through such sensitivity it would seem that we can reach out through the windows of telepathy, clairvoyance and precognition to touch other than three dimensions of consciousness.

First, there is an example of what seems to be telepathic rapport with a living person.

[12-27-'26] — Dreamed Emmie committed suicide.

This shows to the entity, through this correlation of mental forces of the body-mind itself and those of the body-mind of Emmie, that such conditions

had passed through this mind — or had contemplated such conditions, see? They have passed. 136-54

In further questioning the reading emphasized that this attitude had passed. This was checked and found to be accurate. The friend had contemplated suicide. The dreamer could not remember any reason for such a dream. In fact, she had not been in touch with the friend for several years.

In answer to the question as to how this information about "Emmie" was secured by the dreamer's mind, an outline of various types of dreams was given. Nightmares, resulting from physical discomforts; symbolic dreams; problem solving, and psychic dreams were described. Regarding the last the reading gave the following:

Others there are, a correlation between mentalities or subconscious entities, wherein there has been attained, physically or mentally, a correlation of individual ideas or mental expressions, that bring from one subconscious to another those of actual existent conditions, either direct or indirect, to be acted upon or that are ever present, see?

Hence we find visions of the past, visions of the present, visions of the future. For the subconscious there is no past or future — all is present. This would be well to remember in much of the information as may be given through such forces as these. 136-54

Let us turn to an example of a different kind of telepathy. Here the dreamer seems to communicate with her mother who is dead.

[9-5-'26] — My mother appeared to me. She said, "I am alive!"

Edgar Cayce interrupted from the unconscious state saying, *"She is alive!"*

The dream was continued:

"Something is wrong with your sister's leg, or shoulder (or both, I don't clearly remember). She ought to see a doctor about it."

The reading explained this as communication from the dead mother. Included with the explanation was the following:

. . . For, as is seen, the mother, through the entity's own mind, is as the mother to all in the household. Warning, then, of conditions that may arise, and of conditions existent. Then, warn the sister as regarding same. 136-45

So far as this person who had the dream was aware the sister had no difficulties of this kind. However, when this was checked the advice proved to be pertinent.

It is not easy to make a distinction between telepathic and clairvoyant functions of the mind. The fact that these faculties function in the dream state does not make the job of understanding them any easier. Perhaps the best evidence for clairvoyance in dreams can be taken from what are called out-of-body experiences during sleep.

There are numerous sources of reference for such experiences. One of the best known books on the subject is *The Phenomena of Astral Projection*[1] by Sylvan J. Muldoon and Hereward Carrington. Two more scholarly and better documented discussions are to be found in *The Enigma of Survival*[2] by Hornell Hart and *The Belief in a Life After Death*[3] by C.J. Ducasse.

Some aspect of the soul-mind seems to leave the flesh body and move to another time-space. When details of surroundings or actions are noted and recalled to consciousness the observations may constitute clairvoyant perception, i.e., direct apprehension rather than cognizance of thought patterns of another person. In spite of the fact that every one of the fifteen thousand readings given by Edgar Cayce may be examples of such out-of-body experiences, no evidential dreams involving such perception have so far been indexed.

For a typical example of this type of dream experience may I relate a spontaneous case described to me by the participants. Mrs. X, a housewife, lived in Sacramento, California. Her daughter and husband lived in Portland, Oregon. The young people had just had their first child, a baby girl. Mrs. X had written her daughter how much she would like to visit them and see the baby. This would not be possible until spring. On the afternoon of January 6, 1961, Mrs. X lay down in her bedroom in her home in Sacramento. She wished idly that she could see the baby. She relaxed and dozed. Suddenly she was conscious of herself standing in the living room doorway of her daughter's home in Portland. She was aware of her dress, a nice one, not the housedress she wore as she dropped off to sleep. Both her daughter and son-in-law were in the living room. Both of them looked up, startled. Mrs. X awoke in a mild state of shock and confusion. Within a half hour the phone rang. Her daughter in Portland was calling. She was worried because she and her husband had seen the mother standing in the living room doorway. They thought she had died or had an accident. Everyone was relieved and curious about what happened. Mrs. X couldn't remember whether the daughter was able to describe the dress she wore. It would be possible to "explain away" a few such stories. There seem to be a

1 Published by Rider & Co., Ltd., London
2 Published by Rider & Co., Ltd., London
3 Published by Charles C. Thomas, Springfield, Ill.

disturbingly large number of them, and like the above some of them contain evidence which makes too large a bulge under the blanket of coincidence.

We turn finally to the fascinating precognitive type of psychic dream. Philosophically, time is considered one of the greatest barriers to man's perception of reality. Certainly there is much evidence available in the annals of psychical research to show that it is a most confusing issue in psychic studies.

Beginning in June of 1925, and ending in June of 1929, a young woman twenty-one years old secured seventy-nine readings from Edgar Cayce interpreting her dreams. The readings averaged four dreams per reading, a total of more than three hundred dreams. During this period the young woman was married, her father and mother died, a child was born to her and she faced problems with her husband which led to divorce. Her dreams contain what appear to be an amazing number of precognitive experiences. The following are only a few brief references to illustrate the kind of material available for study — and what can be expected from a study of one's own dream record.

June 6, 1925 — Dream of girl friend (self?) at dinner table making violent love to old boy friend.

The reading warned of this problem. Several years later the dreamer asked for and obtained from her husband a divorce in order to marry an old friend. The marriage was never consummated.

June 7, 1925 — Dream of a weak-minded child. (Her son was a mental case 25 years later. In this reading we find the following,

. . . **for dreams are that of which the subconscious is made; any condition is first dreamed before becoming reality.**

July 18, 1925 — Dreamed husband wasn't coming home any more. The reading warned of possible trouble. (Divorce followed five years later).

October 29, 1925 — Dreamed of five chrysanthemums on father's grave. — Reading predicted that in five weeks an experience with the father (who was dead) would occur which would be comforting. This transpired in a dream in the fifth week.

December 27, 1925 — Dreamed sister and self were at mother's bedside. She was unconscious. Both were crying, "Don't leave us." Reading indicated warning of mother's death.

July 17, 1926 — Dreamed of traveling on boat with husband. Lightning struck the boat and the boiler blew up. — Reading warned of the trouble between husband and wife ending in divorce four years later.

November 27, 1926 – Dreamed cousin was married. – Reading indicated that this was precognition. This event took place several months later.

These seven examples will suffice to indicate the kind of material which is available. Fortunately, Edgar Cayce received regular correspondence from the husband during this entire period. He was interested in his wife's dream study. There are confirmations of these and many other points mentioned in this series of dreams.

Here is one final example of apparent precognition. It deals with a well-known historical event, the New York Stock Market crash of 1929.

One of the Association members who was recording and studying his dreams telephoned Edgar Cayce on the mornings of March 5 and April 6, 1929, to recount dreams which he had the night previous. Readings were given to interpret these dreams on each of the successive mornings. This man, whom we will call John Doe, was a member of the New York Stock Exchange.

March 5, 1929 – Dreamed we should sell all our stocks including box stock (one considered very good). I saw a bull following my wife, who was dressed in red.

About this dream Edgar Cayce's reading includes the following:

This is an impression of a condition which is to come about, a downward movement of long duration, not allowing latitude for those (stocks) which are considered very safe. Dispose of all held, even box, signifies great change to come. 137-115

On April 6, 1929 – Dreamed a young man was blaming me for murder of a man. A gang asked, 'Is there anyone else in the world who knows this?' I answered, 'K. Cornell.' Saw dead man. Gang started to administer poisonous hypodermic which had been used on dead man. I felt needle and expected death. 137-117

Awoke and then went back to sleep. Dreamed interpretation: "This represented fight going on in Reserve Board – stock stimulation."

Edgar Cayce reading given same day, April 6, 1929, included:

There must surely come a break where there will be panic in the money centers, not only of Wall Street's activity but a closing of the boards in many other centers and a readjustment of the actual specie – higher and lower quotations to continue for several moons while adjustments are being made – then break. 137-117

On October 29, 1929, 16 million shares of stock were sold. The markets were closed in New York, and elsewhere. Well-known firms were forced out of business. Men committed suicide because of their losses. Banks were closed. We went off the gold standard as a nation. In fact, we had a financial panic which was a forerunner of one of the worst depressions in our national history.

There are some interesting and complicated symbols in John Doe's short dreams. In the first one the red dress might signify danger. The bull might for this man be a "bull market", which was leaving. It was a curious coincidence that this man's wife asked him for a divorce a few months later.

In the second dream the group of men were identified in the dream continuation as members of the Federal Reserve Board. The hypodermic seemed like a good symbol for the injections (support) being given the failing market. Perhaps we can stretch a point and tentatively identify K. Cornell, the admired and well-known actress, as John Doe's higher, or spiritual, self. The attack on John Doe was representative of the loss which was to hurt him personally, as indeed it did, for this man did not accept the interpretations. He did not act on them. The readings' description of "closing boards" "readjustment of the specie," "several moons" of continued fluctation, "break," "panic" were all strong terms. They evidently, at the time, seemed far-fetched. All that we can say is that this appears to be precognition in dreams of a crucial national event almost six months prior to the actual occurrence. Ask yourself, "Do I dream of coming events. Is this possible?"

Spiritual Guidance. — In considering this dream category we may take special note of three major factors: First, symbolism plays an important part in this type of dream. There are fewer instances of direct perception or literal images. Second, we should look closely for symbols of the higher self. At this point it is not important whether you call this an over-soul, super-conscious mind or a collection of high ideals and principles. Third, universal symbols and racial memory patterns are more likely to appear in such dreams than in any other.

The following is an example of this type of dream from the Edgar Cayce files.

April 25, 1925 — It seemed there were two ways of crossing a river, an upper bridge and a lower. And some were using the lower one; so did I, but this time was lying down and traveling right along the water's edge. It seemed dangerous to me, and had to be done often before I had full confidence.

In this we find that a correlation of the physical and the subconscious forces is given; the lessons as given here: The river, the way of life; the passage over, the existence or span through or over which the material man passes in the passage through earth's plane. There are two ways, the higher and the lower way: that in the higher giving the great, broad outlook over the whole of universal forces, that of the lower ever the way of the great masses. 'Choose thou as to whom thou wilt serve.'   900-64

Here is another example which used different but as universal symbols as occur in the one above.

October 25 – Dreamed of riding with someone to the top of a high mountain. There they showed me a beautiful view spread out below.

This, as seen, indicates emblematically (symbolically) conditions in the mental forces of the entity being correlated with cosmic conditions. As is seen, going up the high mountain shows the life (of the entity) in its development of those conditions that give the more perfect understanding of the physical world. The view obtained being, then, as the entity gains knowledge of how to acquire possessions in the physical world or indulge the proclivities in that way and manner in which the world becomes, as it were, dross to the mental forces of the entity, as is seen in that as said, 'Though beautiful – and one gain the whole world but lose his own soul, what is the profit therein?'   341-15

While both of these dreams take on a quality of the conflict between different areas of the unconscious there are certainly admonitions for spiritual guidance in both of them. The symbols too, the river, the bridge, the mountain, all have a universal significance. It may help a person a great deal to come to an understanding of how his unconscious uses these well-known symbols.

Here is another type of dream with spiritual significance:

April 21, 1925 – I saw the world as a great, irregular massive ball, and I seemed to be an entity going out into space and returning to the massive ball, to become a part of the latter, then breaking away again. This was repeated several times.

This again is the exemplification in the material world of the entrance of the superconscious forces into the realms of the subconscious, acting in accord with the higher elements of the mental forces of the entity. Hence the difficulty, the inability of the entity to attain the access attempted. The lesson, then: Keep self in that way and manner so that all of the questions pertaining to the earthly realm, earthly conditions, whether of the physical, mental or spiritual forces, may be accessible to the mental forces of the entity.   900-64

This dream seems to suggest symbolically the tremendous reach of the mind. The dreamer, in this case, had begun studies in the field of psychical research which were both exciting and disturbing.

The dream seems to picture this new mental activity.

Let us consider one final dream experience which had a profound effect on the dreamer. No interpretations from the Edgar Cayce readings are available. However, the person involved has made a continuous study of her dreams for many years. She has a fine mind which is constantly in conflict with her emotional life. In this dream the emotions are caught up in a symbol of high ideals and principles. The result was a healing experience, a spiritual renascence.

"Awoke sobbing. There was a vivid memory of the Master Jesus holding me in His arms. He was seated and dressed in a blue robe. I was overwhelmed with a feeling of tenderness and love. For a period of time following my divorce I had felt lost. Now I felt at peace. It was a strange sensation, for prior to this time I had no personal feeling toward Jesus, no consciousness of Him as a person. This was a turning point in my life."

It would seem that the dream experience can be a vivid and moving one at a spiritual level. Perhaps this type of dream should be distinguished from other types as, in Pliny's phrase, "dreams sent by the gods."

Working With Your Own Dreams

In observing our minds at work during sleep you and I may discover that our thinking is not always what we think it should be. We may also discover that we are far more capable than we ever imagined ourselves to be. Unfortunately, the mental activity during sleep is partially or almost completely closed off from consciousness most of our lives. Assuming for the moment that it may be valuable and interesting to open the door on this world, how can it be done?

The first step is the conscious determination to become acquainted with the unconscious language: "I want to know what my mind is doing while I sleep." With this decision in consciousness, begin at once to think, as you ready yourself for sleep, "I will remember my dreams." Just that. Don't get involved in a complicated suggestion. Simply say over and over to your self, "I will remember my dreams."

This is a positive suggestion to the unconscious mind and, in order to make it work, you must take steps to complete the suggestion so as to affect the physical consciousness. Work with the law of expectancy. Place a pad and several well-sharpened pencils on your bedside table. A little scrap of paper and the stub of a pencil out of reach across the room will only result in your unconscious mind laughing at you or ignoring you altogether.

26

A final step which completes the expectant attitude and is necessary for some people: when you awaken pick up the pad and pencil before you start thinking about whether you remember a dream or not. The dream may be right at the pencil point, so to speak. If you are not accustomed to recalling or being aware of your dreams you may think that these suggestions are like suggesting that you pray for rain on a sunny day and then pick up your umbrella as you leave the house. You will discover that it works better than most prayers for rain. Remember that it is your unconscious which receives the suggestions. It is a sign of disrespect (to yourself), a peculiar kind of self-criticism, to say you do not remember your dreams. You are in fact admitting that you have no idea what you spend a third of your life doing. There is a good chance that the third you are missing is far more interesting than the two-thirds concerning which you have limited awareness.

In beginning the writing of your dream book — for that is what it should become — there are several general observations that may be helpful. Some of these have already been suggested. All dreams are important, but some are far more valuable than others. It may be necessary to record many relatively unimportant dreams before you begin to have access to the more important ones. When you first meet a friend, pleasant but unimportant remarks are exchanged. You seldom get down to serious discussion immediately. Getting acquainted with your unconscious may be like this. Dreams may have several meanings at different levels. For example, one dream may relate to the physical body, your occupation and also contain spiritual guidance. You are the best interpreter of your dreams. Don't take other people's solutions lest you unintentionally avoid facing yourself in a helpful manner. Do not be disturbed by the physical nature, or the frequent sex patterns, of your dreams. Remember you are in the earth in a flesh body which is heir to all the desires and drives of a lower nature. Objective observation will help you understand what you are facing in dealing with yourself. Many people's failure to remember dreams arises from this refusal to admit the existence of this side of their nature. Remember that a good psychologist or psychiatrist might require you to record a hundred dreams or more before beginning to work with you. You are not going to be able to understand your dreams by becoming acquainted with the meaning of just a few dream symbols, any more than you would be able to read a foreign language with a small vocabulary. We must learn the language of our unconscious.

Now let us take a dream and break it down step by step. Several years ago a young man in his early twenties took part in a dream study project in one of our Association summer projects. He became interested in working with his dreams and continued recording them after leaving Virginia Beach. He had the following dream several months after the summer session:

He saw himself standing at the ocean, fishing. The water was clear and beautiful, though turbulent. Standing beside him on the sand was a little figure, not a child but a small replica of himself. This smaller self was weeping. The larger self caught a fish, a beautiful orange-colored flounder. The larger self turned to the smaller self and gave it the fish, whereupon its crying stopped immediately. The flounder flapped and landed in a clump of bushes. The small self began to cry again. The young man began to hunt for the fish. On parting the bushes he discovered the fish being eaten by two animals. On one side of the orange flounder was a beaver and on the other a white rabbit. The beaver ran away and did not return. The white rabbit leaped into the ocean, swam around and came out dripping and bedraggled.

If you had this dream, how would you begin to break it down so that you might understand what the unconscious mind is thinking about? Begin with a question which you must ask yourself many times in working with your dreams: "What does a fish, the ocean, a rabbit mean to me?" Take each symbol separately. Question yourself about it and write down a few phrases about it. Pass over the difficult ones for the time being. Come back to each symbol again and again until you have worked out a meaning for each of the major items in your dream. If necessary, put your puzzle away for a day or two, then come back to it, adding any new meanings that occur to you. Avoid using word associations only; use phrases to describe what the symbols mean to you.

Here are two different day's work on the symbols of this dream which this young man made.

Ocean – I have read that water means spirit or source of life, or the unconscious.

Fishing – Act of seeking in the spiritual realm.

A fish – Something out of the spiritual realm.

The self (larger) – Me as I am now in the physical.

The smaller self – Could this be my childhood? Was I starved or hungry in childhood?

Crying – Part of me wanting something. Stopped crying when got fish.

Fish got away — Lost something which started smaller self crying again.

Beaver — work like a beaver.

Rabbit — timid.

Later the young man went back to the list of symbols above and added to what he had already written.

Ocean — (Add previous data) Later — Whatever ocean stood for, such as spiritual source of life or unconscious, it was beautifully clear, but turbulent.

Fishing — same. Later — nothing more.

A fish — Later — A fish was the symbol used by early Christians. Could this mean Christ, or spiritual food?

The self (larger) — Later — I seem to be seeking, or fishing, as I am now doing in real life, for direction for my life and solutions to my problems.

The self (smaller). Later — This isn't a child. It is an exact duplicate of me. Can this be the part of me which needs spiritual food, small, undeveloped, a part of me that is crying out and is satisfied when given the fish? Maybe this is not my childhood, but rather part of me as I am now which needs help.

Crying — Later — Nothing more.

Fish got away — Later — Somehow, my spiritual food is getting away.

Beaver — Later — When I think of a beaver I think of work. Maybe this is my job.

Note: At this point it would be well to present some background which will help us understand what this young man was discovering about himself through his dream. He was working in a plant making parts of missiles. He was unhappy in his work, for he worried about devoting time to what he thought of as destructive efforts. In working with a group of very material-minded young men he had begun to take on their habits, of dirty language, regular drinking after work, etc. These habits had brought him into conflict with his young wife and an unhappy relationship had developed. In a very real sense, the beaver (his work) was eating up his spiritual food.

White Rabbit — Later — I raised a lot of white rabbits when I was a boy. Sometimes I liked them. A lot of the time it was hard work taking care of them.

Note: It took considerable questioning to help this young man to realize suddenly that the white rabbit might well be a sex symbol for him. "I liked them," boiled down into his observations of the rabbits' sexual habits. He apparently had learned a great deal from the rabbits. His attitudes toward sex as an adult could also be said to be eating up his spiritual food. It is interesting to note that this young man gave up his job and secured another in a line of work which he considered to be more constructive (the beaver ran away). He made a real effort to rethink and change his sex attitudes and habits (the rabbit swam in the ocean and returned to shore.)

In examining this dream and the young man's comments on the symbols it is possible to trace some of the sources of the symbols. Such observations should aid us in dealing with our own dream symbols.

The dreamer's observation on water is classic. In this instance he takes his cue from some of the 600 Edgar Cayce readings interpreting dreams. The fish was taken in an historical sense, through association with the early Christians. Here too the Edgar Cayce readings suggest a meaning which he seems to have adopted — "food for the spirit" or the better part of his nature.

The larger and smaller self are interesting symbols. Of special note is the dreamer's first thought to relate the smaller self to childhood. Here a transcription of the dream, written immediately upon awakening, is most valuable. It would have been easy to have turned the "small duplicate of self" into a childhood image. Thus the parents could have been blamed for neglecting the spiritual training in the earlier years. The modern self would have been freer of current responsibility. The written dream described this small self as a "duplicate of self," not as a child.

The "beaver" and the "rabbit" came from an accepted, well-known phrase, "work like a beaver," and a childhood memory which was at first obscure. The answers to the question, "What does a rabbit mean to me?" gradually brought back the fuller significance of the white rabbit symbol. From this distant vantage point it is possible to wonder about the first description of the rabbit — "timid." How much violence went into this attitude to compensate for this reaction? What is the significance, if any, of the color of the fish, orange? In some systems of thought the color orange might be related to the adrenal glands, associated with both fear and courage. Certainly, it will be helpful to make a note of colors in dreams, especially when identified with particular symbols.

One cannot help letting the mind drift for a moment to one of the most famous of dreams, which has become a children's classic for adults, *Alice in Wonderland.* It was a white rabbit which led Alice, an adolescent girl, down the hole. The passageways she traversed might well be compared to corridors of the unconscious. Surely we are all looking for the garden door into the beautiful place, and we all frequently find ourselves blocked by a physical self which grows too large and too important. And surely we all sometimes almost drown in our own tears of self-pity.

To summarize briefly:

First, suggest to yourself as you go to sleep, "I will remember my dreams."

Be prepared to start writing immediately on awakening. When dreams get too long, brief them. They can be fitted in later if you have recorded the salient points.

Break the dream down into separate symbols. List each one and after it write a phrase answering the question, "What does this mean to me?" Now go back to the dream and put your explanation in place of each symbol. The dream will "open up."

Conclusion

In *The Twilight Zone of Dreams,* Andre Sonnet quotes the German eighteenth century physicist, Georg Christophe Sichenborg, as saying, "Dreams often lead us to situations and circumstances which were we awake, we could approach only with great difficulties. Or they leave us with uncomfortable feelings due to causes which are yet small but which, with the passage of time, could grow to great discomfort. Thus dreams can influence our decisions and can strengthen our moral equity much better than all the formal teachings which have to follow roundabout ways before they reach our hearts."

Here, as in the Edgar Cayce readings, the personal quality of dreams is stressed. In our informal study this personal factor has been noted and stressed by grouping dreams under four broad categories: physical, self-revealing, psychic, and spiritual. Remember that many other classifications of dreams might have been selected according to the particular study being made. All four of our groups deal with personal elements, but, more important, seem to relate to help being given from the unconscious mind. It should not be assumed that all dreams will contain such help. However, it is important to note that the Edgar Cayce readings place unusual stress on this point. Also, there is emphasis on the need for individual interpretation.

The purpose of this study has been twofold: first, to outline ideas in the Edgar Cayce readings on dreams, and second, to encourage you to become a small, one-man laboratory to test these ideas. Here we do not have to depend on theories. It is not a matter of simply accepting what has been set forth. The ideas can be tested. Write your own dream book. Study your dreams as outlined here, and let us know your results. The next booklet we publish on this subject should be written by you. In the process we may discover a new and helpful source of inspiration and strength. Perhaps we can direct this giant within to help us toward a richer, fuller life.

A Psychic Interprets His Dreams

by Tom C. Clark, Ph.D.

The dream is perhaps the oldest psychic phenomenon in man's history. As long as he has slept, man has dreamed. At various stages along the path of his development man has known the meaning of his dreams and been guided by them. At other times the frightening aspects of their mystical content have made him ignore them. It is, perhaps, not without reason that the meaning and significance of the dream is being rediscovered, re-examined, and re-appraised in this most material of all civilizations. Just as it is also not without reason that our greatest illnesses at the present time are mental illnesses and our most progressive and contributing scientists are our psycho-therapists, psychologists, and psycho-analysts, so the meaning and value of the dream as an expression or clue leading to healing, warning, courage or strength, now receives new recognition.

The Old Testament abounds in stories of dreams, dreams of prophecy and of warning. There are many references to dreams in the New Testament also. For instance, in the first two chapters of St. Matthew five interesting dreams are recorded. In the first, after Joseph has found that Mary was with child, he considered divorcing her but then the angel of the Lord appeared to Joseph in a dream and told him that the child was of the Holy Spirit. The second guided the wise men after the birth of Christ, for they saw enough in a dream not to return to Herod but for their safety to go to their own country by another way. In the third, the angel of the Lord appeared again to Joseph in a dream and told him to take the Christ Child to Egypt and to stay there until he was told otherwise, for Herod would destroy the Child. The fourth dream occurred after King Herod had died and Joseph in that dream was told to take the Boy and his Mother and return to Israel. But when Joseph heard that Archelaus, the son of Herod, had succeeded his father, he was afraid to return, and in the fifth dream it was accordingly revealed to Joseph to go to the land of Galilee. These five dreams came at a critical time in the guidance of a great life.

My own longstanding interest in and study of the phenomenon of dreams made me willing to accept an invitation to give three lectures on the subject at a June Congress at Virginia Beach. Most of the material in these lectures came from psychologists such as Freud, Adler, and Jung, and I tried to show the different techniques of dream interpretations as well as the importance of the dream to the individual in aiding him to understand himself or to make adjustment to a problem within himself or others. Illustrative of one unusual method of analysis, I also took several dreams which had been interpreted by the psychic, Edgar Cayce, in clairvoyant readings for people who had submitted their dreams and sought the help and guidance of his information. It was not until after I had finished my lectures that I learned Mr. Edgar Cayce had himself submitted a whole series of his own dreams to his psychic source and had received interpretations of them. The existence of this unusual dream material interested me highly, and I have since spent considerable time studying the complete file of Mr. Cayce's dreams and the interpretations of them he secured.

I found a total of ninety-one dreams thus interpreted. These dreams extended over a considerable number of years, the first recorded one being January 13, 1925 and the last one February 14, 1940, thus covering a span of fifteen years. For convenience in analysis, I sorted them into five different categories.

Kinds of Dreams Studied. — The first general division is between "sleep dreams," that is, dreams which Edgar Cayce had in normal sleep, and dreams which he had while in a psychic state or under self-hypnosis. For it is an interesting thing that when this man put himself to sleep to give a reading the person for whom the reading was given might be in Miami, Florida, while the physical body of Mr. Cayce was at Virginia Beach, Virginia and in the trance state, while his mind was somehow getting information from Florida, he was at times informed by his unconscious in dream. Upon awakening he recollected the dream but concerning the subject of the reading he had no conscious recollection whatsoever. There were only eleven of these dreams in his self-induced hypnotic state, which were later submitted for psychic interpretation, while there were eighty normal sleep dreams.

The normal sleep dreams I further broke down into five different subjects. (1) Work dreams. This word "work" is a term used by Cayce and his associates to cover his psychic phenomenon and all of the activities carried on around it. There were thirty-five such dreams. (2) Personal problem dreams. Into this category I placed dreams about Cayce's troubles and problems with himself, and problems which arose in his relations with others which did not have a particular bearing upon his psychic work. They are about problems of money, of people, of constant moving, and about his development, his weaknesses and his strength. There were thirty-three such dreams. The next category I have designated as (3) sex dreams, seven such dreams. The fourth category (4) covers dreams by Cayce about his physical condition, health habits and illnesses. There were five such dreams. This makes up the ninety-one dreams on which interpretations were secured.

The Psychic as a Man. — At this point I want to say a few words about Edgar Cayce, the man, and what these dreams reveal on his character and personality. Nothing is more illuminating of the real person that lies behind the shallow mask of consciousness than his dreams, and when these dreams are recorded in chronological sequence over a period of years, we see not only the dominant character traits but also their development and changes. Along with the man's weaknesses, fears, doubts, anxieties, hates, irritations, and emotional instability, we see his strength, courage, principles, honesty, trustworthiness, and loyalty. It is all paraded for examination and review.

From one point of view, there is good reason for all of that to be hidden in the mystical language of dream symbols which require patient hours of quiet introspection for the discovery of their real meaning and application. The bald instantaneous truth about ourselves presented at one time would be too great a shock for most of us to bear. But patient digging and examination often turns a cruel fact in our dreams into a helpful solution, just as a large dose of medicine taken at one time may kill the patient but if administered over a period of time, in small doses, it performs a curative miracle.

In the early dreams between 1925 and 1930, Cayce is revealed as struggling and fighting with himself. He had a premonition that what came through him was of a divine nature and his dreams revealed to him that he was anything but a divine individual. He struggled desperately with himself to live by and bring into his conscious life a few divine principles. At one time his psychic source, when asked to interpret a dream, refused the information because, it said, in the past, in connection with similar dreams which had been interpreted, Edgar Cayce had ignored the lesson and done nothing in his life to make correction or adjustment. Even his psychic informant, then, turned against him with impatience and criticism. In certain respects — and unfortunately they were important — he was a weak man, even as most of us in these respects are weak.

After 1932, the content of the dreams started to alter. Fewer dreams were submitted to the psychic source for interpretation and there was evident a definite change in Edgar Cayce's spiritual development. The conflicts and doubts were pretty well resolved and he had a clearer intuitive comprehension of the meaning, importance, and validity of the information which came through him.

I did not know Edgar Cayce in his lifetime and it is not my purpose to use these dreams to pass judgment in any respect upon him. His life work and what he left behind will do that. I cannot leave this subject, however, without stating that despite all of his weaknesses, doubts, fears, arrogance, perverseness, stubbornness, and sometimes downright orneriness, he nevertheless kept and preserved his desire to help people as an ideal throughout his life. This ideal dominated his entire life and although it may at times have been obscured, it was always revived and in the end it was accomplished. He did help people and in addition he left behind a treasure which will be a continuing source of help to those who search for it.

A Psychic's Theory of Sleep — the Sixth Sense. — Curiously enough, for modern psychologists, psycho-therapists and analysts, the study and analysis of the phenomenon of the dream has not carried with it the indispensably related subject of sleep. Dreams that penetrate to our consciousness all take place in the condition of sleep or, we might better say, in that state in which consciousness is absent, for we do know that dreams occur in hypnosis and under various kinds of anesthesia where normal consciousness is dormant. Carl Jung, the psycho-therapist, has made the statement that we probably dream all of the time — in consciousness, as well as when we are asleep — but I think what he calls the performance of dreaming in a conscious state is actually a vision, hallucination or intuitive or clairvoyant perception. It is definitely not the same thing as a sleep dream.

What is sleep? And what is it that occurs in sleep which produces the dream? We must have some answer to this question, or theory about it, before proceeding to an examination of these dreams and the symbolical dream language. Out of the Cayce dream materials come suggestions for a theory of sleep.

Consciousness is a phenomenon supported by a material mechanism. The seat of consciousness is something entirely different from the seat of mind, memory, imagination and spirit. As a purely empirical thing, the neuro-surgeon has been able to isolate a minimum working area for consciousness within a relatively small area of brain tissue, known as the thalamus section. Using local anesthetic, these surgeons have been able to cut off whole areas of the brain without destroying consciousness and with the patient remaining completely aware of surroundings, people and what is taking place, being even able to converse with the surgeons and nurses. Only when this one thalamus section, which comprises an area less than 1/300th part of the brain tissue, is severely injured is consciousness lost. To this extent, consciousness is material and is made up of impressions and reactions from the five senses transmitted through the sensory nerves to the brain.

The five major senses of consciousness are, of course, sight, sound, touch, taste and smell. The combination of these senses with many others on the surface and within the body makes for what we loosely term "awareness" and their operation, consciousness. Now what happens when we go to sleep?

In sleep, these senses are relaxed and in repose. They are not active, although the auditory sense remains on guard. As you know, through whispered suggestion a person may be hypnotized in sleep, but stimulation of any of the other senses will awaken the sleeper and bring back consciousness. It is an attribute of the senses that they produce what is known as perception. Perception is the translation of an impulse transmitted through one or a combination of the senses into an awareness of the thing being perceived. In other words, perception is in itself a sense and, for our purposes, we may designate it as a sort of "sixth sense." We may also safely postulate that this sense of perception, this sixth sense, does not relax or go into repose during sleep as do the other five senses. Let us visualize this sense of perception as being in the nature of a photographic plate which translates sensory impressions into objects. This is the function of the sense of perception and this sense continues to perform that function whether the body is in a state of consciousness or unconsciousness, so long as this sense of perception is activated by other impulses. As you can therefore see, the sense of perception remains aware and continues to function during sleep. However, *in sleep it receives its impulses from the other side, i.e., from the unconscious and from the senses of the unconscious, rather than from the five senses of consciousness.*

Every function of the human body — and this sixth sense is a very important function — has the tools and the equipment with which to perform that function. In consciousness, this sense of perception performs its function chiefly through the use of visual images, the importance of the sense of sight being well illustrated by the expression, "seeing is believing," — or, as they used to say in Missouri but apparently have long forgotten, "Show me!"

Our consciousness is overwhelmed by these visual images, quite often, to the obliteration of impressions from the other senses. In addition, the ability to form images often runs away with us and we exaggerate or cannot recognize an event we have actually witnessed when it is later shown to us as recorded by a camera. Our daydreams are full of visual images and it has been said that, for the majority of us, we think in images. Mention the word "house" and most of you see a house; "dog" and you see a dog; "mother-in-law" and you see her, too. Most of you do not see the words "house" or "dog" or "mother-in-law." You see the objects. These images of every conceivable kind are the tools and equipment of the senses of perception, just as the red corpuscles, white corpuscles, hemoglobin are the tools and equipment of the blood.

We have postulated that this sense of perception, this sixth sense, does not go into repose during sleep as do the other senses; and we have imagined it as a photographic plate on which the image exists, awaiting a stimulant for its illumination. I suggest to you that in sleep that image becomes what we call a "symbol." It is merely our sense of perception employing the same tools that it uses in consciousness; stimulated, however, by the senses of the unconscious instead of the five senses of consciousness.

What are these senses of the unconscious, or better, for our present purpose, what are the senses of the unconscious which produce dreams?

As you will have noted, we are now in an area of theory and assumption where no scientific proof exists and where the test is the reasonableness of the theory. I trust you will not be too critical. At least, you cannot accuse me of abandoning fact for theory, for no facts exist and I believe I am advancing a new theory — every bit of which comes from these psychic readings on the nature of sleep and phenomenon of dreams. You must excuse me if I am not too exact in defining my terms. After all, these are fourth-dimensional, subjective concepts and it is extremely difficult to couch them in our ordinary three-dimensional language.

Three Sources of Dreams. − What, then, may we postulate as the senses of the unconscious which produce dreams? They are three in number. The first and easiest are sensations emanating from a physical condition of the body. Whether we are alseep or awake, the unconscious remains at all times aware of the state of our health, our health habits and also where the body is heading. From this sense come the warning dreams of illness and the good dreams of cure.

The second sense is what we may call the *mind of the soul.* Fortunately, we do not have to defend the existence of the soul. That, at least, we may for the present accept, but we do have to assume that the soul has certain elements and it seems to follow naturally that if we have a mind of the body, we should also have a mind of the soul (as the Cayce materials suggest). This mind of the soul is our inheritance from the past and our link with the future. It is what we have been plus all of the urges, ideals and searchings of the present. This soul mind is a "sense" and it registers its impressions, its judgments, its evaluations, warnings and praise upon the film of perception, producing the symbols, or images, just as do any of the physical senses. This sense produces our dreams about ourselves, our struggles and frustrations and our external adjustments or lack of them.

The third sense that produces dreams we may describe as a spiritual force or as a sense emanating from the mind of the spirit. This is the area which Jung has called the "collective unconscious." It is the unifying force in the universe where the unconscious of each and every one of us meets with its colleagues. Dreams from this sense are more in the nature of visions, and proud may be he who has been spoken to through dreams from this sense. Apropos is the quotation, "And their young men shall dream dreams, their old men shall prophesy and their maidens shall see visions."

From the foregoing we can see that the dream is either (1) a reflection of the physical condition of the body, or (2) a judgment with respect to the activities of the individual or conditions surrounding him, or (3) a projection from a spiritual force. For the purpose of analysis and interpretation, I suggest that all dreams may be divided into these three categories.

The Language of Dreams. − The origin of the dream symbol probably goes back beyond the origin of writing; indeed, may have furnished the basis for it. At least we know that our earliest written language was a pictorial one in which a sign or symbol stood for anything from an emotion to an object. Consider for a moment the difficulty man first encountered in expressing love, hate or fear in a picture. And how would you pictorially express an ideal or a purpose? In our dreams this is very clearly and easily accomplished. For instance, we dream about a person we dislike. Actually, what the dream is featuring is our feeling toward the person rather than the person. We dream about an animal, let us say a bear. Actually, we have not dreamed about a bear at all but rather about what that bear stands for in our estimate of the characteristics, instincts and habits of the bear. (In passing, I may say that the bear is often a mother symbol of not too healthy content, for bears are known to suffocate their young with an overdose of affection, a trait not unobservable in some human mothers. Be careful with your dreams about bears!) At any rate, our earliest written language consisted of this kind of pictorial symbol with symbolic meanings. And then came the myths.

In the images of mythology — and mythology is practically all-symbolic — we have a wealth of material for the discovery of the meaning of dream symbols. Believe me, our dreams use these mythological symbols in abundance. The Gordian Knot, the labyrinth of Mimos, the snakes of Medusa, the dolphin, Prometheus chained to the rock, Pegasus, the flying horse, the apple and the serpent, and so forth. Examples are almost limitless and each symbol has its definite assignable meaning dependent on the context of the dream and the problem to which it relates.

I believe it to be a rule that in a general way we can classify all our dreams (except dreams involving the physical condition of the body) into two categories according to the symbols used. (1) If the symbols employed are taken from nature, i.e., trees, animals, roots, mountains, water, rivers, deserts, clouds, etc., our dream relates to an internal problem we have with ourselves. It is about our attitude, our development or lack of it, our unhappiness, our purpose and our ideals. (2) On the other hand, if the symbols used are manufactured objects such as houses, carpets, pictures, money, trains, automobiles, dishes, locks and keys, etc., our dream relates to an external problem involving some marital, social, economic or other problem requiring adjustment. These two general categories while not infallible, provide a useful guide in the interpretation of dreams.

It is entirely possible that additional classifications of dreams may be made, through further work in sorting out dream symbols according to the kind and type of animal and plant life portrayed and the kind and type of manufactured articles. For example, there is undoubtedly a distinction between the symbol of a work of art, a statue, painting, or example of classical architecture, and a symbol of a modern ranch house or ordinary brownstone. The real self is buried so deep in the unconscious that the variety of symbols used by it for its expression is almost infinite and can become exceedingly obscure. Thus, the art of correct dream interpretation requires a high degree of skill, for the interpreter must not only be able to identify the symbol but also to know the mythological or other background comprising the story or stories in which that symbol has been employed. In the psychic interpretations which we will examine, that knowledge appears to be instantaneous and complete; at the same time the source provides a correct application of the symbol meanings to the problem dreamed about.

Up to now we have explored a theory of sleep and how the dream occurs. We have advanced a theory of the source of the dream and we have very briefly looked at the nature of the dream language, symbols. We go now to a brief review of the modern psycho-analytic understanding of the dream, in comparison with the concepts of the psychic, Edgar Cayce.

Psychic Parallels to Jungian Psycho-analysis. — As with practically everything else in psycho-analysis, we find that Freud was the first to use the dream as an expression of the unconscious. In a very short time he solidified his theory about the dream and — as with practically everything else he developed — he stuck with that theory (or on it) for the remainder of his life. Even though it was shot full of holes, he nevertheless, about fifteen years after originally announcing it, wrote another paper reaffirming his original contention.

According to Freud, the dream is nothing more nor less than a suppressed wish and all the symbols in it, in one form or another, relate to some sensual, sexual or carnal impulse. No one denies that there are such dreams, but no one except the ardent followers of Freud — of whom there are many — has the audacity to maintain that all dreams are of this character.

Adler ascribed even more importance to the dream than did Freud and discovered in it support for his theory of the will or desire for power (or adequacy), as well as evidence of Freudian sexual urges. Each psycho-analyst who has developed a theory with respect to the nature of psychic maladjustment has similarly found support for his position in the dream symbols until we now have as wide a variety of dream interpretations as we have theories about the nature and cause of psychotic and neurotic manifestations. Among all of these scientists of the soul, Carl Jung makes more use of the dream

41

in his psycho-therapeutic technique than any of the others and the phenomenon of the dream has accordingly received its greatest study, analysis and development from his work and that of his pupils. Dream analysis is the principal remedy or medicine which Jungarians use in their therapy, and it is exceedingly interesting that the meaning assigned to symbols, the method of dream analysis, and the purpose ascribed to the dream function, as formulated and advanced by Carl Jung, are all closely similar to those found in the dream interpretations by Edgar Cayce's psychic informant or source.

Water — life, the living way.

Fish — Christ, Divinity.

Fish — breaking of — giving of life.

Fish — a lesson in life.

Size of Pen and Size of Ink Bottle — indicates importance of transaction.

Theft of Closed Dish — represents taking of control into his own hands rather than consulting openly with others.

Hammer — a driving force.

Bull with a Queer Head — hardheadedness, stubborness.

Carpet — to tread upon, walk over in an unseemly manner.

Flying Feathers — commotion and confusion.

Three Steps — the three-fold way of life.

Drunkenness — confusion and dissension.

Exchanging Old Suitcases for New — means "take not of that which is new until you have completely absorbed and used that which has been lived and is true. Don't be fooled by appearances."

Locking Back Door — the desire of the physical body to shut out unpleasant conditions.

Opening Front Door — receiving spiritual assistance.

Hog — take over, dominate.

Peacock — false front for self gratification.

Negroes — a stage of mental development.

Drawing of Water — taking from the water of life, the word and work of Jesus.

Court Room — "immature concept of Justice."

Craziness and Idiocy — a position or attitude in which others hold the dreamer — out of reason.

King Solomon — wisdom, or to seek wisdom or truth "but also to abjure the weakness of the flesh represented by him."

Band of Gold Cloth — the preciousness of the proper ideal.

Wall — obstacles in the physical body to the acceptance of a new ideal.

Fall and Cry of a Woman — "Beware that the thought, the intent, the purpose of the entity is not shadowed by success, fame, glory and gold".

Nudity — exposure of self, consternation and confusion.

Sinking Floor — poor foundation for ideals and principles.

Dining Room — source of food for thought.

An Enclosure or Fence — a field of endeavor, activity, life's work.

Animals — characters in people; stages or states of their development; their dominant characteristics; fundamental and basic elements of their personalities.

Goose — constancy in affection and marital relations.

Money — rewards, compensating factors.

Scissors or Shears — "Most symbolical implements to man of life and death."

Saddle — to ride with, make adjustments to, fit and cooperate; not run or steer.

Head on Backwards — preconceived ideas prevent proper understanding.

Shiny New Coat — anger and bad attitude.

Snake — the wisdom of all things which leads to temptation.

Camping — change of location, moving from one house to another.

Trap — snares and pitfalls in life, errors, wrong attitudes.

Drawing of Blood — either destructive or life-giving, dependent on other conditions and associations in the dream.

These meanings and this technique of interpretation closely parallel the work of Carl Jung. The similarity is striking and exciting. Jung came by his theories through years and years of study, vast erudition and masterful scholarship. Hundreds, perhaps thousands, of patients paraded through his consulting room and filled his

43

clinics with every sort of mental illness and, also, every kind of normality. Out of that wealth of experience and his extensive studies, he evolved his theories and, believe me, they work. On the other hand, we have this psychic gift or power of Edgar Cayce, instantaneously producing similar findings for patients with an authoritative precision that demands action. Jung can only infer, suggest and recommend. But in either case, you take the consequences. In the last analysis both counselors end with the same injunction, for both say that only through the Word of God can man find happiness on earth and eternal peace.

The Process of Getting the Interpretation. — I have listed only a few of the several hundred symbols which appeared in these dreams, with the meanings ascribed to them by the psychic informant. Please note two important points. *First,* some of the symbols belong only to the individual dreamer. They are *his* symbols and have a particular meaning for him. On the other hand, a few of the meanings given for these symbols do have a wide applicability, such as those for water and fish, for example. *Second,* the meaning or shade of meaning for a given symbol may change, depending upon the other symbols in the dream and the problem with which the dream is concerned, for example, the symbol of blood.

I mention these cautions about interpretations, for some of you may want to study your dreams, and I highly recommend that you do. Put a note book by your bedside and write them down the first thing when you wake up. If you misinterpret and make application of the misinterpretations, look for another dream soon to follow which will correct your interpretation and again try to show you the right way. You will not be censured by your unconscious for the misapplication but you will be censured if you don't listen to your dream and then act upon it.

Remember, in this connection, that the only time Cayce's psychic power refused to give an interpretation of a dream of his, it gave as a reason that Cayce had not applied the lesson of a previous interpretation and acted upon it. You pay for your sins of omission, while the others may be forgiven!

The dreams were interpreted in the same manner that all other readings were given. He lay down and went to sleep. One of two kinds of suggestions might then be given. If the dream to be interpreted had been written out, it was verbally suggested that he should give an interpretation of the dream had by him on a certain date which would then be read. However, it sometimes happened that Mr. Cayce neglected to write out the dream or had forgotten

44

the details. In this case the verbal suggestion was given that the dream had by Mr. Cayce on a certain date involving a horse or the climbing of a mountain, or whatever be recalled and interpreted. There are a number of such interpretations in the file I studied, and in such cases it is impossible to reconstruct more of the dream than is indicated through the symbols which were interpreted.

Sometimes the whole recorded dream was read before any interpretation was given. In a few such cases, after the entire dream had been read to him, the psychic source commented that some very essential and important parts of the dream had been omitted and then gave those parts! Frequently, they were of an uncomplimentary nature, the omission of which would be quite understandable. At other times, with merely the date of the dream having been given, the interpretation would start immediately, without any of the dream having been read, even though it had been written out in full.

At still other times when the reading of the dreams had proceeded about half way the interpretation would start on the part which had been read but also that part not read, as well as on the insertion of other parts not included in the written statement. As mentioned, there was only one instance in which an interpretation was refused and then for the specific reason that Cayce had not acted on previous interpretations in his daily life.

One Dream and its Interpretation. — We turn now, and finally, to our examination of one of the dream readings of a psychic with its psychic interpretation.

Edgar Cayce's dream reading December 6, 1926:

Yes, we have the body, the enquiring mind, Edgar Cayce. This we have had before.

The dreams, as we see, come to the entity in the way and manner, or through one of those channels as has been presented: that is, the conscious visions or conscious conditions made applicable to the conscious of an entity, through the process of the subjugation of the conscious bodymind by sleep.

Ready for dream.

Q-1. Saturday morning, December 4, 1926. I dreamed I had an enclosure in which there were all manner of birds, beasts and fowl, with a large, high wire fence around these. I noted especially there were a bear, goat, sheep, deer, goose, fox, wolf and dog. The dog was one I knew. I was feeding them, and I realized that it took different feed for the various kinds of fowl and beasts that were there, but at the time I was feeding shelled corn. A few grains went through the fence, and I saw the goose and the wolf go through the fence, but I

45

couldn't understand how they went out, and then came back in after getting the few grains. While stooping I heard and saw a commotion among all the animals and birds. It seemed like a warning cry, as if each in its own language was trying to tell me I was in danger. I realized it was a bear behind me, but I thought, a bear doesn't do anything but scratch or hug one to death. I glanced over my left shoulder and realized the bear was sitting behind me, on its haunches, with its forearms or paws outstretched. The dog, the goat, and the deer sprang to scare the bear away. In a flash I wondered if the bear meant harm or did he mean to caress me. I woke up shaking.

A—1. In this there is presented a vision of far meaning to the entity, when properly understood, and many various phases of the entity's endeavors are visioned in the presentation of this to the entity.

The enclosure represents that condition hedged about by the entity's field of endeavor – to be of assistance, aid, help, to others – and in same there is seen all manner of beast and fowl and birds. Some especially are noted.

For, as seen, each animal, each bird, each fowl, has been so named for some peculiarity of that individual beast, bird or fowl, and in this manner represents some particular phase of man's development in the earth's plane, or the consciousness of some particular element or personality trait that is manifested in man.

Not that man develops from the animal, or the animal develops from the man but as has been given, all beasts, all birds, all fowl, were made for man's use and sustenance. Hence each must supply, in name, manner, position in life, in its phase of living, in its habits, in its conditions, associations and relations, some element that is necessary for man's development.

In this phase and in this light, then, we find the entity, the individual, supplying that food for the development of mankind, in mankind's personaltiy. And all are seen represented, as noted by the individual that various phases of the vegetable or animal world are necessary for the full and complete development of the animal or fowl that is to be sustained.

This is seen in the casting of corn, or that which is a necessity to animal, or fowl. As some grains pass through the enclosure it is seen that some words spoken by the entity are as the casting of pearls before swine, going beyond the reach. Yet, as seen, two creatures which represent different phases of man's consciousness, or man's personality in the earth plane – the goose and the wolf, are even able, though cast beyond their reach – to reach same. How this is understood, or how this is reached, is that which troubles the entity. And as the entity stoops to see, to understand how these animals or fowl pass in and out, or gain access to the knowledge, or gain a portion of the knowledge that is received by that cast, there appears the heavier beast that to others, those about

46

it – would appear to do harm.

As seen again, in the nature, the character of the beast itself, it presents a phase of development to the entity regarding certain individuals, or a certain class, that would act in a manner such as this beast does regarding the information or the truths or the lessons being cast before these for their sustenance. There is seen in the kind of beast – represented by the bear – one which would under certain conditions be very destructive, under other phases of its consciousness playful, and as caressing and as loving and as tender and as protective to the best interest of the individual in every way, as would any of those who come to the individual's assistance.

Yet, as seen, when there is the fear of destructive forces there are especially three characters that rise to the defense of the truth. One in the form of the dog (which represents a certain nature, character, or disposition) the other in the deer (which represents another form), the other in the fox and wolf (which represent still other forms). Some would save for self, yet would be destructive to others. Some are as one protecting that which it loves, that it may not destroy itself, see? These are the characteristics, the elements, the conditions.

This is a beautiful lesson, to be studied hard and much may be gained therefrom. For it will be found the basis of something that may be used as a lesson to many.

We are through for the present.   294-87

You will note in the above dream some of the symbols previously referred to, such as the enclosure or fence being a field of endeavor or life's work, and animals which represent stages or states of development in people. Note also the expression "casting pearls before swine," and the symbolical manner in which that expression is presented.

Two Other Dreams Interpreted. – An example of a physical condition dream and the interpretation of it is found in the following, dated December 30, 1925:

Dream: Dream of being crazy and of looking into my head and fixing a wheel that had stopped running, owing to a particle of dirt or trash getting into it.

Interpretation: This is a subconscious vision of physical conditions existent in the body, and is presented to the body in this emblematical (symbolical) form to indicate that through the condition seen, the eliminations are poor in the system, producing a pressure on the nerves that give, as it were, motion to the action of the brain force, and in the removing of same (poor elimination) there is seen the works, as it (the brain force) goes on. Then (here is shown) a purely physical condition needing repair, in a way as presented – oiled up, or lubricated–

47

that the drosses may be removed from the physical body, that the excesses of dross be cleansed, so that the brain may function normally.   294-56

An example of a dream and its interpretation with respect to certain activities in Mr. Cayce's life and how he was advised about them through dream interpretations is found in the interpretation to a dream which occurred on April 15, 1926 and is as follows:

Dream: Dream regarding fixing over an old house, about a watermelon eating a pig.

Interpretation: This, as we see, is an emblematical (symbolical) condition to the entity, and shows how the entity should study those conditions.

As seen in the vision or dream these things could not be true from the conscious position. Yet there is preparation by the entity to build on same.

It is further presented that the entity is preparing to make a firm foundation, or feels that is is so − over that which is rotten, and which is eventually shown even to contain dead men's bones!

There is further shown that (instead of) the hog attempting to eat the melon, which would be normal, the melon eats the hog, or pig. This shows the unreasonableness of conditions being presented. And any attempt to build upon same comes to the end which is seen − in the sinking of the floor over which there had been the contemplated floor for dining room.

Then, the entity should take stock of self, and know that there may be certain conditions that enter into the life, from certain elements, which may not be stable and which may not be builded upon in a way and manner which will bring the very best to each.   294-72

The three dreams quoted above are typical examples of the material found in this file and show not only the meanings ascribed to the symbols but also the interpretations of those symbols as applicable to some current problem then facing Cayce in his life or activities. I believe we may safely conclude that these dreams − and they are fair examples − are no different from the dreams that come to most of us.

Conclusion. − In one of his latest books, *Essays on Contemporary Events,* Jung has a chapter on Wotan, the Norseman's God of War. In that chapter Jung tells of his work with a great many patients during the period 1935 to 1939, particularly his patients from Germany, and the dreams they dreamed. To his astute observation, the cataclysm which fell upon the world for the next five years was not startling or a surprise. What happened, though it happened to the mass of people and not just to a few individuals, Jung saw in advance in the

48

pattern of sick attitudes and ideas repeated over and over in his German patients.

Today it is profoundly disturbing to note that such sickness is still widespread, both here and elsewhere, though we continue to believe that confusion exists only outside of us; that it is only the neighbor or the neighboring state that is evil; that no war or conflict can be allowed to end without an army of occupation and the full, absolute and complete eradication of any and all resistance whatsoever. I venture the opinion that if we could assemble the dreams of a cross-section of our people, particularly those in public life, and expose them for examination, we should know beyond the shadow of a doubt not only why we are in our present mess but where we are heading. Truly, man walks in his own shadow and in these times man seems to have decided that truth lies only in the atom bomb — or with him who has the most of them. In other words truth is physical power, overwhelming physical force, and in this scheme of things there is, of course, no place for the still small voice of our dreams.

What an apt parable we find in the story about Elijah! You will remember that after he had challenged, defeated and then slain the 450 false prophets of Baal, Jezebel threatened to kill him and Elijah fled across the desert to the mountains and hid in a cave. The Lord then came to Elijah and said "What dost thou here, Elijah?" Then he told the Lord of the reason for his flight and the Lord told him to go and stand on the mountain and he did. On the mountain there came a great wind that threw down the rocks, but the Lord was not in the wind; and after the wind there came an earthquake which shook the entire firmament, but the Lord was not in the earthquake; and after the earthquake, a fire, but the Lord was not in the fire; and after all the tempest had passed, there came a still small voice that said to him, "What dost thou here, Elijah?"

So we would do well to ask of ourselves: "What dost thou here?" "What are your purposes?" "What are your ideals?" "What are your goals?" and listen to the still small voice in our dreams. It will help us to find our way.

Working With Dreams As Recommended By The Cayce Readings

by Shane Miller

Method of Procedure — While it remained for Freud, Adler, and Jung to awaken us to the importance of our dream life as a gauge to the state of the subconscious, time may show Edgar Cayce as the man who took dream interpretation out of the hands of the "experts" and restored it to the individual, where it belongs. For out of the Cayce readings comes a working premise so simple in its essence that through it hope may be brought to any individual who earnestly desires to stand on his own feet.

The Cayce premise states in effect that anyone, whether physically gifted or not, who will record his dreams in an attitude of prayerful persistence can, in time, bring about a complete restoration of the dream faculty. (The dream faculty at present seems to be the remains of a long disused and discredited function of the higher mind.)

This is the first half of the premise.

The second half states as simply that the best interpreter of the individual's dream is the individual himself, since the symbols are his own. As an additional explanation, the readings point out that when dreams are fragmentary, disjointed, and without a clear motif they are likely to be the results of faulty digestion or other physical disturbance. On the other hand, any dream which has a certain "story" content or mood, particularly if it is in color, should be studied. And that is the complete premise which, if *faithfully* followed, can bring a new dimension into the experience of anyone who will keep "everlastingly at it!"

50

By the same token, anyone seeking a new quick easy road to "illumination" is eliminated by the stress and strain of the discipline implied. Discipline is usually rather uncomfortable and troublesome. Who wants to be uncomfortable?

In doing research upon the dream premise, the neophyte finds certain discrepancies between the methods recommended by Cayce and those of science. Basically, the scientific approach to research of any kind is one completely unbiased by the personal opinions or feelings of the researcher. The ideal for the man of science is complete detachment; the attitude must be impersonal. On the other hand, the Cayce position is revealed by one word contained in the second paragraph of this report. That word is "prayerfully" and that makes the Cayce approach very personal indeed!

The lay investigator of psychic research is not overly concerned whether certain phenomena have happened or can happen. What he wants to know is, "Can these things happen to me?" If the results are beneficial he will probably apply them in his daily life. If he cannot use them, he is not particularly interested in adding to the sum total of human knowledge per se. It must be useful in some way to him. It must be practical in his own terms. Ideally, the Cayce lay investigator goes to his task on a basis of prayer and meditation, not asking that great shiny miracles happen but that the "right" things happen. There is nothing impersonal about it.

As General Heard once expressed it, "How does the 'fact-and-figures' man know what the object of his search may think of *him* and *his* efforts?"

Without the humility of this attitude, the investigator cannot hope to penetrate very deeply the levels and reaches of the human mind. Unless this point is established early, nothing that follows in this writing will make sense.

The first explanation along these lines, in the A.R.E. Center in New York, took place in 1952 as a group enterprise, for the purpose of solving a common problem. The work was begun with a clear statement of motive and purpose and, since the situation held a certain urgency, there was emotional involvement also, according to the depth of the individual need.

Prayer was the means to be used in bringing about the adjustment of the situation, but since meditation for guidance was a novel concept to many of the group, the use of dreams for guidance was agreed upon as a psychic faculty which lay within the reach of most people.

The activity of this group did bring about a generally improved situation, as it happened; but with regard to the dream project, many had fallen by the wayside. The keeping of a dream record is a form of discipline, however slight, and discipline, as we have said, is a great deal of trouble.

Perhaps it should be pointed out that the subconscious is the seat of all habits, good or bad. In working with the subconscious to replace a bad habit pattern with a good one, the desired pattern must be instilled, through repetitious ritual or corrective action. The subconscious thrives on monotony — and this is the nature of all disciplines.

Most of us in beginning the dream experiments had long lost the ability to dream at all. Tension and struggle had made us too exhausted to dream. We began by following instructions literally, by first placing a pencil and notebook at the bedside and inaugurating a new *habit* of prayer for the restoration of the old function which had been missing in some of us since childhood.

Dreams began appearing in fragments, with now and then a longer episode with a more definite pattern, but we could not yet read the symbols. Doggedly we put them down and let them "cool." They were entered in the book with the date and the word "analysis" after it, where the interpretations should go. Wide margins were left wherein we could list the symbols. In this way slowly but surely we developed a kind of vocabulary by which we could translate the dreams into everyday English.

The point was to keep going, in all patience, no matter what happened. *Dream symbols have a way of changing with the growth of the individual.* This is a most important point, since the subconscious mind is not all hedged about with the fixed standards and yardsticks of the conscious mind. The subconscious, like the ocean, moves with the tides and rolls with the punches, so to speak. It is in a constant state of flux. For example, if I dream of a specific house known to me in my waking moments, my first impulse is to identify the dream house literally with the actual three-dimensional house of my acquaintance. Perhaps I dream that there are termites gnawing at the foundations of the house and I might even hurry over and find the termites actually there and hard at work. A year later, however, I dream of the same house and the same termites. This time, however, I sense that the house is only the symbol of the condition of my being. The termites gnawing at the foundation of this house now indicate that my condition of well-being is undermined by hidden worries and fears.

Now both of these interpretations, one of the direct literal, and the other symbolic, may be strictly correct. The whole message of the dream might be shown to read, "In the same way that the old Jackson house is being slowly consumed by termites (literal) you are being undermined by your own petty fears and annoyances (symbolic)."

Yet each of these interpretations is sufficient unto the development of the individual at the given moment. The factor of growth has given the deeper interpretation; greater possibilities become apparent and the consciousness expands. For the person of fixed literal ideals and standards this state of "relativity" is extremely hard to understand. That's why it is so necessary to persist. How many people in the world are said to be able to understand Einstein's "Theory of Relativity"?

(Also, since much of the Bible is written on a number of levels in a like manner, an understanding of dreams and their laws is of great help in understanding the Bible's vast scope.)

When dreams begin to come in color, adding a new dimension to what has gone before, it seems to me that such dreams have a spiritual source. Dreams that look like tinted photographs — light washes in color — are of the mental and the dreams in black and white are physical. In any instance, moreover, where there is difficulty in interpreting either the symbols or colors — since these have meaning too — there is nothing to prevent the individual from asking to have the dream shown again in terms he can understand.

The greatest thrill, the greatest sense of wonder, comes from the experience when the individual discovers that throughout his researches he has not been alone! Like the little boy who took a long pole to measure the depth of the pool at the bottom of the garden he finds each day that the pool shows a different depth. Shortly afterwards he makes the great discovery. There is Something or Someone on the other end of the pole moving it up and down!

We have not been *alone* all this time!

This is the part of the story which is extremely personal. It is also very difficult to write. In an effort to simplify this point, since the point in essence is simple, I will merely call this the discovery of the figure I think of as the "Man."

The "man" is a figure who appears in my dreams, the figure for whom I never fail to look. He is usually shown in some position of authority. At other times he speaks in words that seem to sound only in my ears without his taking form, usually to explain some point. Once he appeared as an army colonel out of uniform, implying that he could suggest but not command. However, no

53

matter in what form he appears in a dream, I can always recognize him by one thing. That is my vast sense of love and respect for him, a kind of tearful happiness in his presence.

John, in the Book of the Revelation, speaks of a figure he calls the Ancient of Days, a figure which so over-awed him that he wanted to fall down and worship him. The figure earnestly warned him against this, saying "I, too, am a slave" meaning that he too had form.

Seemingly, this is the "elder brother" the Christ speaks of in the parable of the Prodigal Son, the brother who never left home. This is the real *I* who never left the presence of the Father and through whom my prayers are offered − a real guardian angel, perhaps, who is in charge of this fragment of individuality walking around in the earth plane. And yet so jealously is the factor of Free Will guarded that the "man" will not even offer help unless I ask for it.

"Whatsoever you ask in My Name, believing, that will I do!"

On June 15th, according to my dream record, I awoke with these words ringing in my ears.

Ah, well, I told you this would be difficult to write.

Understanding One's Own Symbols

Ideally, the purpose of analyzing one's dreams is to make a beginning of bringing into *conscious* experience all levels of the human mind through knowing their laws of operation and the nature of the contents. Knowing what is in the tool box and how all the tools work, we will agree, would make a fine beginning, but other factors enter the picture − unforeseen factors which are the result of growth.

During the period of fragmentary dream experience encountered by the beginner, the symbols are usually accepted literally, since the average man is used to thinking in that way. Then as symbols appear which are part of group or folk ideograms, the individual becomes aware that he has tapped a deeper level of the mind, what is known as the "collective unconscious." The eagle appears in his dreams, perhaps, as a high flying ideal, the lion symbolizes strength and courage, an old bearded man in classic robes is wisdom incarnate. These are symbols, to be taken literally.

The thoughtful man now goes back to his earlier dream recordings with their literal terms and interprets the objects he has seen in them as symbols of states or conditions occurring within himself. A new lucidity springs from the pages. Many times the way in which a condition is reported will be the clue to what part of the body, mind, or spirit is calling for attention and corrective action. As color is added, and contact established with the highest self, one's education can really begin in a consistent fashion. One begins to work with that part of the self which is closest to the Universal Forces.

This, in general, is the pattern of progression of the dedicated man who sets himself to know himself in patience and prayerful persistence. What form his "education" will take depends mostly upon his urgent need, that need which has emotional content. The following is an account, from my own dream record, of a cycle of dreams which had its beginning in a personal way and led into what turned out to be a kind of lecture course on Life after Death.

Three days before my father's death, in 1953, I dreamed that a woman appeared to me on the staircase of his home in Philadelphia. She said, "I come to offer condolences on 'the death,'" and continued on her way upstairs. End of dream. My father had been ill for some time; the end had seemed imminent time and again, but when I went away for the weekend of that week I took enough clothes with me to see me through a possible trip to Philadelphia, in case the warning was realized. No time of fulfillment was given, but the Cayce readings state that in many cases the deceased will appear *in a dream* to the loved ones to reassure them, *after* three days.

In a general way I reckoned the time of Dad's death to fall on Saturday; in this case, three days after the warning. The news came at 5:30 p.m. on Saturday and the following day we left for Philadelphia directly from there, exactly on schedule. (This is an example of a simple prophetic dream.)

I found that my father had died in a coma, that he had passed on without knowing what was happening. The third night after his passing came and went without a dream of any sort. On the fifth night I had a dream which showed him sitting at a table, with his back toward me, as he fitted the *pieces of a jigsaw puzzle* together. The anagram suggested two things immediately: first, that he was unaware of my presence, and second, that he was trying to figure out *what had happened to him!*

Months later, at lunch with a friend, I was discussing the matter of prayers for the dead. The friend, as a young man, had been educated for the priesthood and his explanation for the reason and function of prayers for extreme unction and for the freeing of a soul from purgatory gave me a new understanding of the subject. His explanation was given in terms of modern psychology rather than religious ones, since I am not of the faith. It ran about as follows:

In depth the individual releases his hold on the conscious mind, which is the seat of free will. In giving up the will the consciousness "relaxes" into the subconscious, which is without free will. Here the soul could remain for a long time, trapped in its own thought forms, desires, and old habits. Ultimately the soul will discharge its mental "desire-waste," after which it can rise to its proper level in the spiritual hierarchy, or the "Mind of God."

This period of involvement in the "inter-between," so to speak, can be shortened by the prayers of those still living in the earth plane, still in possession of conscious will, such as family and friends. Prayers for the dead are a concern in the Jewish belief as well as the Roman Catholic teachings; only the Protestant group seems to make little of prayers for the dead, once the funeral is over.

As a Protestant, therefore, I had perceived through my dream researches that my father seemed to be having difficulty; certainly he needed guidance of some kind, for although he had been a religious man all his life he had never shown any disposition to comprehend much beyond a three-dimensional nature. The "theory of relativity" would be beyond him by far, even though he was now living in the state of being where "relativity" was the condition whether he could *understand* it or not. He was a traveller in a strange country without knowledge of the law, language, or customs.

Quickly I made use of the services of a group who offered their prayers for him, and in subsequent dreams I witnessed a steady progress in my father's condition, until now it has been a long time since I have dreamed of him at all — which I take to be a good indication of his development.

However, at the same time, through my concern for my father and its emotional accompaniment, my dream experience widened out to include a series of dreams that would explain the general state of Life after Death. Two of the dreams are given here.

These dreams showed that the "inter-between" and its conditions and laws were pretty much as my Catholic friend has described them, but added a factor. It was demonstrated that "free will" was still possible but that the modus operandi was different. Much would depend on what instruction a man had before his death which would enable him to understand the after-life and its laws and how to work with them. This is not to say, on the other hand, that a "shrewd operator" with the lore of the subconscious state at his fingertips could twist his way through the obstacles and "climb into Heaven some other way." Nothing of the kind.

The dream shown me to illustrate the nature of this "inter-between" state was given in the form of an "assignment," so to speak, as if I had been a schoolboy! It follows, as I wrote it down in my dream record under the date December 12, 1953:

"This was a dream in which I was fully conscious that it was a dream. There was a small room, on one side of which was a kind of lunch bar with several people at it, myself included. Significantly, I understood that it was a 'middle room' — that there were two others that it led into and out of. (Doors on either side of room.)

"Near the door was an object which I understood was an old-fashioned sewing machine. It was made of brown walnut, with the case covered with a number of bumps and knobs. I concentrated on this machine, resolving to register its contours exactly so that I could draw a picture of it afterwards. This I found I could not do, since I could not bring it into clear focus. Each time I tried to see what any one shape was, it became any shape I had preconceived it to be! Thus it appeared in a continuous state of flux.

"Resolved now to relate this experience to John (my Catholic friend) when I saw him again, I tried another experiment. This time I tried moving the machine — it looked to be very heavy — into a corner of the room. I tried to levitate it over an endtable that was in the way, but I couldn't manage it. However, when I looked away from the corner of the room which was the goal point of the experiment, I found that the sewing machine was snuggled up against the endtable, having moved a distance of about six feet during the time that my *attention was off it!"*

The Subconscious Does Not Want to be Spied On. — This "middle" room, I understood, symbolized the state of the soul immediately after death, showing both the advantages and limitations of the soul's new expression of will. The symbolism indicated that it is an inter-between condition (two doors) and that the souls are fed (instructed) here before going on. The objects in the room were concepts abandoned by the soul's passing through. (The symbolism is, of course, my own.)

Now, the other dream, to show perhaps that the dream state and the inter-between are one and the same. This is another "assignment" dream, dated January 16, 1954.

"I walked between two cottages, built on a hilltop, that were tied to each other by a porch looking down on a wooded slope. The trees were in full color, and I said to myself: ' Ah, it's Fall — and it is because I wanted it to be Fall, which is my favorite season. It's Fall because I willed it to be so.' Down the slope was a very lovely and solidly-built house about which a number of people were standing or moving. I decided to go down and see what the inside of the house was like. Obligingly enough, a stairway formed for me, leading down to the level where the house was. This gave me the clue that I was . . . in a dream and I said to myself aloud.

" 'This is a dream, obviously. I will walk down the steps and in so doing prove that *willpower is a factor in the dream state as well as the physical.'*

"I tried to go down the steps but I *simply couldn't move!* By the time I gave up I was lying on the stairs head downward trying to crawl down with all my strength, using fists and heels. I simply could not do it . . . *Once I had given up,* however, I looked at the house, longing to see inside it, and — zip! there I was inside (the house) with all the people who lived in it."

To walk down the steps would have been an act of will, which is the property of the conscious mind only. The simple unexpressed *wish,* however, placed me inside the house instantly, without involvement in *time, space, or motion.* One scene merely faded and the new one of the interior came on. This illustrates the working of the subconscious mind.

The stairway appeared in answer to a wish, because I *believed* it was a necessary means of getting where I wanted to go. I could not move because *motion* has a *time* factor, but with the desire or wish, all obstacles were hurdled *instantly.* This region was peopled entirely by my own thought forms and acted only in response to my unexpressed desires. Moreover, they acted in *expected* patterns. However, if my father had appeared to me here, as well he could have, his actions would have been his own and might well have been at cross purposes with me and my expectations. Yet such a factor gives the clue by which an individual recognizes whether the loved one he seems to be meeting is genuine or only his mental concept of the loved one!

The Master must have smiled when He said: "In My Father's House are many mansions — "

Extracts from the Edgar Cayce readings on Dreams.

. . . The study of subconscious, subliminal, psychic, soul forces, from the human standpoint, is and should be the great study for the human family; for through self man will understand his Maker when he understands his relation to his Maker. He will understand that (relationship) only through himself, and such understanding is the knowledge which is given here in this (psychic) state.

Each and every person getting this understanding sets his individual force toward the Great Creation; and has his individual niche, place or unit to perform (fill). (Each individual) has to reach (understand) numbers (varieties) of psychic forces or phenomena that may be manifested in the earth plane . . . Yet the understanding for the individual entity, viewed from its own standpoint, with its knowledge, is obtained and made ready *by itself,* to be manifested *through itself, towards its own* development; and in that the entity's development (affects) the creation or world. In this manner, and in this form, and in this way, will the development be of assistance to the world.

As in dream, those forces of the subconscious when taken or correlated into forms that relate to the various phases of the individual give to that individual a better understanding of self, when correctly interpreted, or when correctly answered.

Q—44. How should dreams be interpreted?

A—44. This depends upon the physical condition of the entity and that which produces or brings the dream to that body's forces.

The better definition of how the interpretation may best be (made) in this: Correlate those Truths which are enacted in each and every dream. . . Use them towards the better development, ever remembering "develop" means going toward the Higher Forces, or the Creator.

Q—43. What is a dream?

A—43. There are many various kinds of manifestations which come to an animate object (or being which is in the physical plane of man) which the human family terms a DREAM.

Some are produced by suggestions which reach the consciousness of the physical through the various forms and manners (such) as these:

When the physical has laid aside the conscious in that region called sleep, or slumber; when those forces come through which the spirit and soul have manifested themselves, and are re-enacted before or through, or by this soul and spirit force; when an action is of such a nature as to make or bring back impressions to the conscious mind in earth or material plane, it is termed a dream. This may be enacted by those forces that are taken into the system, and in the action of digestion that takes place under the guidance of subconscious forces, become a part of that force through which the spirit and soul of that entity passed at such time. Such manifestations are termed or called nightmares, or the abnormal manifestations on the physical plane of these forces.

In the normal experience of dreams are enacted what may be the fore-shadowing of conditions, with the comparison by soul and spirit forces of the conditions in *various spheres* through which this soul and spirit of the given entity has passed in its evolution to the present sphere. In this age there is not sufficient credence given dreams; for the best development of the human family requires greater increase in knowledge of the subconscious soul or spirit world. This can be gained in dreams.   3744, A-41

Exploration in Depth

— So far, we have dealt with aspects of the dream which are more or less traditional. From this point on we shall encounter some of the less well-known symbols found in "analysis in depth," which the Cayce premise makes possible. If the symbols now seem more and more outlandish it might be helpful to study the classic dream forms and interpretations found in both the Old and New Testaments. Examples are given in *Genesis,* chapters 37, 40, 41 (Joseph's dreams and his interpretations); *Ezekiel; Daniel,* and others of the Prophets; plus the *Book of the Revelation,* which is all in dream symbology. These show the underlying form of the strange (to us) logic running through all dreams.

First, however, let us restate the purpose to be served by a dream analysis made by the dreamer himself, which is according to the Cayce admonition. This purpose is (at least to begin with) *to bring all levels of the human mind into conscious experience, by applying the laws of operation and studying dream content.* Let us know the nature of the "tool box" and how some of the "tools" work, which have been lying idle so long in the depths of our beings!

In the previous sections we have attempted to list three general areas of the mind and their laws — conscious, subconscious, and superconscious — by reporting personal experiences in each area. One facet of this exploration reflected the possibility (not a new idea) that *the dream world, the subconscious levels of mind, and the first stages of life after death are one and the same.* The Buddhist teacher, Chen Chi Chang, in his lecture given in New York under the auspices of the Association in 1955, expressed it in this way:

"He who remains in control of his dreams, in dreaming, is in control of his states of being in the after life."

To proceed to our next point of inquiry: Is it possible, through dreams and dreaming, to review past conditions of the soul, with particular reference to "past lives," which might disclose incidents of former ages which are adversely affecting our present experience?

If so, this dream analysis-in-depth — a fantastic depth by present scientific standards — could put the individual again in control of his destiny as he once was in the so-called "Golden Ages" of the past.

Since Edgar Cayce, the outstanding psychic of our age, gave the subject of reincarnation much time and consideration, shedding new light on its validity and setting forth its relationship to the ideal of redemption as contained in Christian thought, this is a most important field of research. *Many Mansions,* by Gina Cerminara, presents the Cayce viewpoint with such impact that it has inspired independent researchers in the field of analysis in depth. A research of special interest is the exciting new experiment in deep hypnosis recorded in the book *The Search for Bridey Murphy* put out by Doubleday. This is particularly significant in that both author Morey Bernstein and his subject Ruth Simmons are laymen.

However, most laymen researching these areas would like to know "How can this, or its equivalent, happen to me? How can this aid me in becoming a better whatever-I-am?"

The dreams that follow here are presented to show a single experience in this type of research. This is another example of dreams appearing in a cycle or series, to illustrate a certain condition and furnish insight on its possible origin. The cycle came in response to a definite prayer for information about the cause of a condition, which manifested as a kind of perpetual state of frustration. Certain economic commitments were obstructed by this frustration and so there was also an emotional involvement.

The following is taken from my dream record under the date of February 22nd, 1955:

"I was riding on some kind of transportation which I thought of as a trolley car, but which went along the sidewalk and up and down the curbs with a neatness and dispatch . . . (description indicated a wandering course.) At the car-barn at the end of the line I made . . . a complaint to the motorman, who was motorman-conductor combined. He seemed angry when I held out my watch to show him that the trip had taken too long — that we were long overdue.

"He was eyeing my watch — a Gruen wristwatch — with interest, and said that he was much interested in watches. I told him I carried three watches and hauled out the other two (different types.)

"The motorman took all three of them, saying he wanted to look them over, that he would return them to me later. I walked around the car-barn, meanwhile, looking at things.

"When the motorman returned, he handed me the three watches so encrusted with filth and rust that I could not tell them apart! When I protested, the motorman said angrily, 'Those are the watches you gave me! It isn't my fault they look like that!' "

The symbology in this dream is almost elementary. Progress in development and growth is unsatisfactory; there are too many meanderings and side excursions. The trolley car affords a kind of charade of the emotional expression of the prayer upon retiring. In whatever way I had phrased it, it was emotionally the complaint of a weary man. And so the complaint reached the "motorman-conductor," or the superconscious, in the dream. Not much can be done because of the condition of the instruments in hand, the message seems to read.

The watches are the instruments we use to record time. The superconscious examined three of these records, returning them to me in a state reflecting their condition of abuse.

To me, this meant that there were the records of three "times," or lives, which were influencing the present unduly by reason of their unreleased tensions. (Note, however, that my mentor gave me back the watches to cleanse!) One of the watches I had held in my hand. This implied that the present life was one of those needing revision. The other two had been buried in pockets – deep in the soul's past. This in turn implied that two more dreams were to come. I would get the whole story, I reasoned, if I could compare the three experiences in a waking conscious analysis.

The second dream occurred on March 2, 1955:

"Dreamed that I was with a group of people who were looking through a kind of window, a kind of long window seen in broadcasting stations that separates the control technicians from the performers.

"The window looked in on a large room richly furnished and well lighted. The people with me were all in modern dress – evening dress, mostly. (We seemed to be expecting a dramatic performance.)

"I went into the room seen through the window, and a crowd of people came in, all dressed in what I understood to be court costumes in France about the year 1789. (When I looked up this date later I found that it was the year given in the encyclopedia for the beginning of the French Revolution.)

"I myself was in a cream-colored suit with a periwig, knee breeches, etc. I went to shake hands with my 'host,' which, I recalled upon awakening, was not the custom of the times. I could not shake hands with him because his thumb was held well down on the palm of his hand. (I was somehow greatly embarrassed by this in the dream.) I took his hand (in spite of this), shook it, and backed away. He gave me a huge grin and I saw that he was - - - (an outstanding American figure in politics today); seemingly, in the dream, he was a powerful duke or prince of the land. The duchess, his wife (seemed) . . . very angry with him. For some reason, everyone in the room assumed mournful attitudes and poses while they waited for the outcome.

"I sat down near (the wife) and a maroon-colored ribbon fell from (the region of) my right ear into my lap. I sat there waiting for something to happen, assuming the mournful attitude of everyone else, but idly admiring the color combination of the maroon on the cream-colored suit." End of dream.

The fact that people in modern dress were watching the drama through the window indicated to me that all the people present in this 1789 episode are living today. The "duke" would not receive me on my own terms so I backed away like a servant or courtier. My rich clothes showed that I must be a courtier and all through the dream I felt that I must somehow please these people, even to acting out a mood I did not feel in order to *appear* in complete harmony with their mood of the moment. Actually my feeling toward them was complete indifference and boredom with them and their problems, whatever they were. As a courtier my very livelihood would depend upon my ability to anticipate the mood of my superiors and reflect it accurately in my own attitude. There was nothing belonging to me here; I had no stake in any of this. I was a puppet.

Even my implied death at the hands of Madame Guillotine left me completely unmoved and indifferent. Even in the dream I recognized the symbology of the maroon ribbon. It was the color of dried blood, symbol of a past condition.

Three nights later, on March 5th, the third dream arrived. This one had its setting in a castle in Scotland — symbolized by the Scotch burr in our voices as I have set it down here. I awoke from this dream in terror.

" . . . We were sitting at a table in a medieval castle. Mother and (brother) were present. (Mother and youngest brother in present life. Brother was evidently the oldest son in the Scottish lifetime. I was the younger, then.) My brother went to say grace before eating and my mother clawed at my arm saying:

" 'But, laddie, ye'll no be sitting down to meat in full armor when they say grace?'

(In the dream my arm was clad in chain mail. A coarse cloak of green-brown heather mixture was thrown over my shoulder.)

"I had been expecting a guest, a Viking seemingly, of whom none approved. I tried to quiet mother as I bowed my head and my brother delayed grace to wait for the interruption to stop . . .

"(Brother) said, 'Twere best your Viking friend should not sit down to meat in this house.'

"I said, 'Be still, the both of ye, and get on wi' the grace. We canna delay another moment.'

63

"Mother said, 'But, lad, there's a bur-rnin' on your cloak. I'm thinkin' ye'll bur-rrn up, if ye no tak' heed!'"

"As the smoke started up I peeled off the cloak and they soused me with buckets of water. As I hung up the sodden cloak, Brother said, "There's the marks of the burnin' and they'll no brush off. Ye'll carry the marks on the garment all its days!'

(On the cloak were the marks of two eyes, elongated, slitted, yellow, like the eyes of a cat, which I sketched on the page when I awoke.)

"By this time I was terrified (in the dream) and let the cloak hang on the peg. I didn't want to touch it, thinking it full of malevolent forces. Some invisible creature had stared at me so hard that its eyes had burned prints of themselves on (my cloak). Such was my understanding in the dream.

"Just then the Viking came in and in my terror I roared at him: 'Ye'll no be sitting down to meat in this house, lad, for there's summat that'll no let ye 'bide here. Look at the cloak!'

"The cloak reared up of itself (it looked like a green-gray cobra) and lunged at him as he passed it where it hung on the wall. He recoiled in horror and in stentorian tones I ordered him out of the house, saying in a long tirade that I was not willing to risk . . . the cloak's displeasure on his account, now that it was seemingly haunted." End of dream.

To come at once to the crux of this tableau, the symbology tells the story of a "possession." This is not "obsession" in any sense, where the individual is possessed by an idea of his own. The story here is one of a body being taken over by an outside entity while the rightful occupant stands by and watches the proceedings.

Let us be clear about one thing. These dreams are not literal flashbacks of two incidents widely separated in time and space. These dreams, too, are given symbolically.

For example, the Scottish burr reproduced here serves only to identify the country in which the incident took place. The actual language of medieval Scotland was probably a collection of Pictish and Scottish Gaelic, completely incomprehensible to the layman today. Likewise, the costuming, the settings, as in the French dream, serve only to give an approximate date in history of when these things happened. All this is given in the language of dreams — the symbols — which like anagrams are read more readily as practice is gained.

Parts of the interpretation I am not giving here for lack of space. To follow out the trail of symbols leading off through the metaphysics of "sitting down to meat" with a Northman implies a project in itself. Since the Northmen have been shown by history to have been traditional enemies of the Caledonians, as the Scots were anciently known, it was doubtless a serious matter. Certainly the moods and faces in the dream betokened that.

However, just what have these dreams in common? What basic condition do they all contain in the final analysis? For example, what does a French courtier have in common with a Scottish fighting man of the medieval period, a man "possessed of a demon," so to speak?

A man not in full possession of himself cannot act in *Free Will*, because the factor of *control* has been taken away. Free will implies, moreover, *responsibility*. To illustrate: In a moral sense, no soldier can be held responsible for his deeds if he acts according to the orders of his "superiors." Neither can a hired courtier — nor a man *possessed*. Loss of free will, in the Scottish period, conditioned the second or French experience and led to the third, which, by the anagram of the errant trolley car, depicted a lack of drive, of direction, in the present.

As the Elder Brother in the dream pointed out:

"There's the marks of the burnin' and they'll no brush off. Ye'll carry the marks on the garment (soul) all its days."

Shortly before leaving New York in 1939 for a five-years' sojourn in Florida, I visited a doctor for a checkup. He suggested that I take a basal metabolism test. Today, in the light of new discoveries, the metabolism test seems to be more or less out of favor. However, for what it is worth, this test showed that the thyroid was distinctly "below par." The Cayce material states that the seat of the WILL is the thyroid. If this be so, then the implication of the dream shows that a scar left on the soul in ages past and not cleansed or healed, can sooner or later work into the physical and, out of its context, interfere with the soul's progress.

The diagnosis seems complete. The cure now must lie within me, if the diagnosis came from me. The thought is better expressed by the Cayce reading:

Yet let this be understood: No experience, no urge, no environ may be greater than the *will* of an entity. For the *will* — the Creative Force promised in Him — may overcome, may change, may alter that which may come to pass in the experience.   487-17

Contacting the Overself

— At this point in our study certain questions which have been bubbling up during the preceding parts must be dealt with. A summary of these questions might be expressed in a general way as follows:

1. Since the subconscious is suggestible, how do you know that the subconscious is not furnishing the desired dreams in terms of what the dreamer would like to believe? How do you separate wish fulfillment from the facts?

2. If a person is well versed in history, costume, and folkways of the past, isn't it possible that the subconscious is releasing into the dream that which the individual has read and studied in the present, instead of reviewing an actual previous life? How can you tell?

3. If a loved one has passed on, how do you know that your dreams of him are not just wish-fulfillment brought on because of your longing to see him again?

All these contingencies are possible, of course, when the dream is not conditioned by an individual's prayer to the Most High God, whatever that may mean to him in whatever his state of development. Once the prayer is offered and released inward through the emotions, the superconscious is witness to the act. This brings us again to the study of what was referred to as "the man" in Part I, signifying Superconscious Mind personified.

"The man" symbolizes that part of the individuality which did not take part in the "Fall of Adam" — the soul's experience in materiality. He remains "before the Throne," so to speak, to keep open for the adventuring soul the way back to the Creator. He is a witness to the activities of the soul in the earth but he takes no active part, being the Watcher, the Guardian Angel, the brother who never left home when the Prodigal Son set off on his travels, in Jesus' parable.

This symbol of "the man", or John's figure of the "Ancient of Days," found in the *Book of the Revelation,* is beautifully defined in the work of the New York A.R.E. Study Group's study of the *Book of the Revelation.* This figure is described as "the self-conscious, individualized portion of God that is the unchanging core of each entity, whose mind constitutes the Superconscious Mind of Man." He stands at the gateway as a perpetual intercessor between the individualized portion of man in the earth and the Universal Forces.

This intercessor is the part of my individuality which sees to it that any and all information given to me in dreams is according to the needs of the soul at any given moment. This superconscious is the portion of God that oversees the facts presented in their proper order, in symbols of my own educational background and understanding at the moment. This is the part of Me who notices when my consciousness is being expanded and who rephrases the symbology accordingly. This is the portion of my being which stands in the position of Reality, at a time when the rest of me is sunk in the Maya or the illusion of earth consciousness in material expression.

And yet "the man" — the superconscious — cannot act until I ask for help! This is his only limitation — this is his law, as laid down by the Father from the beginning . . .

In examining the two volumes of my recorded dreams, begun January 24, 1952 (this is being written in December, 1955) I found that recognizable symbols of "the man" — the Overself, or Over-Soul — had appeared fifty-four times by actual count. I have listed thirty-six different roles he has assumed, despite which and because of which he is recognizable. (It is most important to recognize the dramatis personae of our dream world, since in this way we learn what parts of the human mechanism are being heard from.)

Here are some of the forms mine have taken:

1. A rider in cowboy costume shown in perfect control of a high spirited horse. (Later the horse was offered to me to ride. All new harness, saddle and stirrups were shown.)

2. Four times as an "elder" brother.

3. Twice as a beloved editor.

4. Twelve times as a "voice", speaking but without form.

5. An ancient ferryman with the archetypal white beard.

6. Twice as an efficient manager of a plantation and a farm — "where everything grows."

7. A floorwalker in a huge department store.

8. Master of a great house (who was asleep upstairs, while I moved around downstairs.)

9. A chauffeur.

10. A man looking at me through the finder of a camera.

11. Elevator operator.

12. Twice as a naval officer and three times as army officers (possibly reflecting problems centered in the Leyden and adrenal centers.)

13. Pilot of plane, conductor of trolley and train or conveyances. White-bearded in most cases.

14. A quiet youth, who could speak French and acted as an interpreter.

15. Proprietor of stores, restaurant, hotel.

16. A young well-set-up physical culturist by the name of "Bestley" (!) who was in firm charge of a whining invalid.

17. Twice as a pastor, once as a surgeon and doctor respectively, once as a school teacher.

All of these are recognizable earth forms or robes. Insight on the superconsciousness' role may be gained by study of an excerpt from a reading:

For the superconscious mind becomes the mind of the soul, in those interims (in the mental planes) between material manifestation and cosmic or universal manifestations – yet these are one. 3605-1

In looking over the list above it is interesting to note the ideal of responsibility reflected by each symbol. In each there is the unmistakable stamp of the custodian, the steward, the man in charge. Toward each one in the dream condition I felt a powerful sense of trust, admiration, and love. But more than that, there was in each symbol a demonstration of what the psychologist today might describe as "moral sense." This seemed to be on the level of "morality" and "ethics" – not so much in a temporal as in a universal sense.

An excellent example of this kind of "morality" – for want of a better word – is the story of Jesus' actions at the wedding feast at Cana. Jesus, with complete understanding of all factors involved, seen and unseen, acted instantly, according to the need of all levels of consciousness and being. He replenished the wine jar. On the other hand, the "good" man whose sole acquaintance with "virtue" had come out of what he had read and held in common with the beliefs of his times, accrued through exoteric religious activity, without firsthand contact, might have responded quite differently to the situation at Cana. He might have spoken a fine little homily about the evils of strong drink, might have quoted from the Bible itself to make his point that "wine is a mocker, strong drink is raging," etc. – and think that he was doing the Will of God.

These are examples of a "temporal" brand of morality, developed perhaps through a study of what *man* thinks God would like him to think in thinking about God. The morality of the Super-conscious or Overself, on the other hand, is on the level of the Christ consciousness; it springs from the knowledge that comes from an uninterrupted contact with the Universal Forces, or God, throughout the ages.

This source of help, information and guidance — the Overself — is within the reach of anyone who will seek. Herein lies the answer to most of the questions posed a while back, since our premise is this: when an individual starts his search to know his relationship to the Universe and its Creator he can expect help from the "other side," as it were, in dreams. He can count on the protection and guidance of this elder brother through all explorations in the wilderness of his mind and heart.

When that contact is established, in some way recognized by the individual, true-self control can begin. In the dream episodes we have related a situation was presented and the cause sought through two past lives. (The emotional response to the situation of the cause was actually powerful enough to make me leap out of bed!) However, a review of the patterns of this (Scottish) life showed that such bizarre effect must have had a bizarre cause. The procedure was orderly and went straight to the past without getting involved in the past ages themselves, with their wealth of interest and detail.

The "sixty-four-dollar-question," however is this: "How can one know that this recurrent figure of the Overself is not a figment of the imagination or another fabrication of wish-fulfillment?"

My answer to this is that when I started recording my dreams I did not expect to encounter such a figure. I did not know he was there. As many times as I had read the *Book of the Revelation* as a boy, the "Ancient of Days" held no personal connotation for me. My reading about "angels", guardian or other varieties, had been extremely sketchy and completely traditional. I had heard that there were "angel hierarchies," of course, and I understood them to be rather like cosmic trouble-shooters, scattered throughout our Universe. I certainly did not expect to meet an angel or angels in my dreams!

The "angel" or figure that I did meet was not always as proud of our relationship as I could wish. He scolded me, "kidded me along" when I was low in spirits, and was most loving and appreciative when I had somehow earned it. His attitude was many times that of a strong man, who, never having touched liquor himself, was somehow saddled with escorting home a brother who had absorbed far too much. Always careful to proceed at the speed of the stricken one even though he knew the way, his chief concern, it seemed, was for this charge and sometimes that charge would get embarrassed and angry. On the other hand, I never could understand what I had done to win his approval, upon those occasions when he did show such.

This is hardly the picture of any kind of "angel" I had ever read about or imagined. Assuredly it is not exactly my conception of wish-fulfillment, either!

"Why is it not possible to use auto-suggestion instead of prayer before going to sleep?" might be another question.

This is possible, of course; and auto-suggestion can sometimes be used advantageously in matters of routine. In important situations, however, the individual many times needs more wisdom than he has on hand; and guidance and protection are needed even in prayer. Here is a case in point, where a friend we'll call Jones appeared on the scene with an idea for becoming rich and successful by establishing control over the subconscious mind through auto-suggestion alone. (This was a personal observation of an experience.)

It sounded fine to hear him tell it but somehow it left me greatly disturbed. When I went to bed that night (July 25, 1952, according to my dream record) I put the following question, submitted with my prayer before falling asleep.

"What is the nature of Jones' new system? What is the truth of it? How are we deceived by it — if we are?"

The answer came, verbally, in dream, as follows:

"The soul takes action on whatever Jones tells it. If Jones' basic premise is off, then the answer is off. Yet the soul mind operates in triumph and in confidence — answering as Jones wants it to — not necessarily in accord with Universal Truth but only in accord with the truth Jones wants the truth to be."

In the three years I have been watching what happened to Jones as a result of his "system," it is needless for me to say that Jones is not rich and prosperous, neither has he established control over anything. As in the case of Fibber McGee's closet, every time Jones pried open the door of his subconscious for purposes of his own, a few more tennis rackets and old shoes fell out! Nevertheless he still thinks the idea is good.

Advice given in the Good Book runs like this: "Seek ye *first* the Kingdom of God and His righteousness and all else will be added thereunto."

An extract from the reading of Edgar Cayce points out a way to do this:

A study from the human standpoint of subconscious, subliminal, psychic, soul forces, is and should be the great study for the human family. For through self man will understand his Maker when he understands his relation to his Maker. He will understand that (relationship) only through himself, and such understanding is the knowledge given here in this (psychic) state. 3744-A-41

Project X Experiments

by W.N. Petersen

For two consecutive summers, the Association for Research and Enlightenment sponsored what is now widely known among the members as Project-X (August 11–31, 1950) and Project-X (August 6–25, 1951).

The projects had specific aims, and certain goals which the participants strove to attain. For a moment, let us re-examine the purposes of these experiments.

The major purpose of the projects was to examine and test the validity of the Edgar Cayce records relating to psychic sensitivity and the possibility of developing it. Psychic sensitivity actually pertains to the three-fold man: the physical body, mental body, and the spiritual body; hence dream experiences were chosen as measuring rods for growth of this sensitivity. The author has broken down the over-all patterns of the projects into these three aspects, and the reader will note later how the dreams expressed themselves in these three realms of activity.

To give a general outline of these three realms of activity:

The Physical

The participants were given sweat baths, massages, sandpacks, and other kinds of physio-therapy. They took a drug known as Atomidine, for gland purification and stimulation; and used a radio-active appliance to equalize circulation and relieve nervous tension. Each individual involved underwent a strict diet, and absolute fasts as particular times during the project. Lastly, Lapis stones* were used as a possible stimulation for glandular activity.

The Mental

An important aspect of the Project was the mental response to the psychological testing, and this was used as a clue to understanding the personality structure. Another critical factor was meditation—each individual going inward for self-analysis . . . to seek and find idiosyncrasies of the personality. Still another factor was the response to music used during meditation.

Mental attitude toward the other participants and toward the all-important work projects was also noted. And lastly, but possibly the most important, was the mental attitude of each individual toward the periods spent in prayer and meditation. All of these activities must be included as aspects in the mental sphere.

The Spiritual

There were really only two major divisions in the realm of spiritual endeavors. First was that of prayer and meditation, which includes meditation for healing; secondly, spiritual law was presented to the groups from various approaches to determine which method might be most practical. The application of spiritual law in everyday activity was stressed.

Spiritual endeavors must also be considered the ultimate goal of the entire activity and the reason for the very existence of the projects. It was part of the project theme, and the target at which the participants were aiming — development of the spiritual man.

The criterion for evaluation of progress and development was dream-recall and dream-analysis; since dreams were a means by which we could note gradual changes, if any, in each domain of influence as the projects progressed.

Two other points need to be noted before going into the meaning of sleep and of dreams.

It has been previously mentioned in other articles, giving quotations and hypotheses based on the Edgar Cayce records, that psychic sensitivity is basically related to the spiritual nature of man; and that this sensitivity functions through the endocrine gland system of the human body.

If we accept this theory as a possible explanation of psi (psi

*Lapis Lingua (referred to as Lapis) means literally tongue stone or talking stone. It was the term used in the readings to designate stones which are a corrosive product of copper in its natural state. The two types of Lapis used in these experiments were: The blue Azurite lapis [2 Cu Co$_3$. Cu (OH) 2], and the green Malachite [Cu Co$_3$. Cu (OH)$_2$]. It should be noted that the lapis lazuli is a different stone from these.

meaning the entire ESP process), dreams involving telepathy, clairvoyance, precognition, and religious experience could be a normal action or reaction of these spiritual centers. In the realm of psychic experiences, there may not be any line of demarcation between perceptions of the conscious and of the unconscious states. If psychic energy flourishes within the one source — that of the gland centers — it would be inadvisable to draw a line just because one facet of the mind is awake or asleep. In fact, we are apt to have more experiences in sleep or unconscious states, for our own ego is resting; our repressions, suppressions, and inhibitions are somewhat released and may manifest in dreams, or step aside so that our higher nature may function without obstruction.

Only one other point should be mentioned before continuing: that of the psychological and mental attitudes of the participants.

Remember, during the first week, negative personality patterns of each individual were deliberately brought into the open. The director, Hugh Lynn Cayce, purposely tried to create confusion, anger, frustration; and to instigate other actions that would be antagonistic. In the dreams of the participants during the first week of the projects, therefore, states of confusion and other emotional attitudes may show very clearly.

During the second and third weeks, which were devoted to positive thought and action, manifestations may also show in the dreams of the participants. Thus we should find less confusion and greater clarity in the dream expressions. Here, then, we may discover what growth of the spiritual body has taken place.

The seven participants in the two projects were asked to keep an accurate account of all dream experiences. From their journals, the author will select examples of the various types of dreams, and trace any subconscious patterns which presented themselves during the progress of the projects.

The reader is asked to bear in mind that these dreams are not actually being interpreted, for the dreams belong to the dreamer. They are merely being classified through observation and speculation. Such an approach is used in order to determine whether the dreams are physical, subconscious, or superconscious in origin or essence.

For the moment, let us confine our observations to dreams that manifested during the first week of Project-X, as recorded by the seven college-age participants.

First Week

A's Dream Experiences

Physical: o. Subconscious: 8. Superconscious: o.

This young man does not appear to have any dreams that could be classified as undoubtedly physical or superconscious; however, we can note immediately the recurring subconscious symbolism. On four different nights he dreamed of being chased or becoming involved with policemen. The symbol of guns and policemen appears quite important to this person. As examples from his journal, we find:

8-12-50 "Some men were chasing me, policemen. I finally got away from them and met some friends who asked me to join them . . . "

8-13-50 "Gangsters and policemen were fighting it out for possession of a house. The policemen won because of a machine-gun . . . "

8-16-50 "I was a detective tracing down my clothes. I threw a police cordon around a house of smugglers and opium dealers. The police pulled a surprise raid, and I was unfairly implicated, even though I knew all about the racketeers . . . "

It would be unwise to classify this symbolism, other than (speculatively) that police could mean authority, and A is rebelling against something of that nature. Another recurring symbolic image is that of money, which, in the readings, has been interpreted as compensation.

On the basis of this reflective observation, we may arrive at a speculative conclusion; namely, that A's dreams reflect a subconscious conflict in some department, and he is looking for compensating factors. The reader will recall the notations in the introduction, to the effect that emphasis was placed upon negative personality patterns during the first week in order to bring them closer to the surface. After they were brought to the surface, they could be examined and then dispelled. Therefore, A's dreams may be the manifestation of pressure applied upon negative factors.

B's Dream Experiences

Physical: o. Subconscious: o. Superconscious: o.

The second participant, B, did not record any dreams in the first week, on the basis that he could not recall any to consciousness. We will, however, note some interesting entries by B in the second and third weeks.

C's Dream Experiences

Physical: 2. Subconscious: 14. Superconscious: o.

Upon examining the journal of C, we find that he dreams on the average almost three separate and individual dream contents per night. Even though the experiences are separate, the subconscious appears to have related one to the other, in order to complete the trend of submerged thought.

C dreamed of having meat for a meal on two separate occasions. These were especially noted, when the fast periods were in progress. The last three days of each week were fast periods.

In the domain of the subconscious, we find our first psychic dream experience: that of clairvoyance. This naturally is not the only true psychic experience of the participants, but one of the rare examples which we have been able to verify. Here is the extract from his journal:

8-12-50 "Was standing by the hedge and saw little girls coming out of the house to play with a group of little boys that were in the back-yard. A little girl dressed in a pale violet dress seemed to be the leader. An argument ensued with another little girl in yellow, as to who would be the leader. After a while they again played games . . . "

At the time of this dream, C did not know that the house in which he was staying was used every fall as a children's school. The kinder-garten-age groups did play often in the yard surrounding the building. C's dream appears to be a clairvoyant experience that manifested while in the unconscious state.

Another sub-classification of the subconscious manifestation which was noted in C's notebook was the type that we could term a dream of solving a problem.

8-14-50 "Had collected different kinds of bottles and took them to the store for refund. The clerk gave me four one-dollar bills for the empty bottles, much to my surprise. Then I went out and tried to find some more . . . "

Notation by C: "Due to the repetition of this dream a week previous to the beginning of the project, I will try this method as a means to gain money which I badly need."

C also has a very interesting recurring symbol, that of washing and drying dishes:

8-11-50 "D and I were in the kitchen washing and drying the dishes . . . "

8-11-50 "The group and I were on our way to a restaurant where we were to clean up empty and dirty dishes . . . "

8-16-50 "I was alone in the kitchen looking at the stack of dirty dishes, and then went about cleaning and polishing them so that they would be nice and shiny. Clean again . . . "

The only explanation the author can arrive at is that C is going through a process of self-examination. He is aware of the need to purge or cleanse. To the dreamer, though, there may be an entirely different meaning.

D's Dream Experiences

Physical: 3. Subconscious: o. Superconscious: o.

The three dreams recorded for the entire week appear to be on the physical level, though they do seem to entail mental conflict on the Libido level of experience.

E's Dream Experiences

Physical: 2. Subconscious: 5. Superconscious: 1.

8-12-50 "Dreamt of strawberries and ice cream, also of radishes, but had the impression that I should not eat them . . . "

The other physical dream also contained food items.

E was contemplating marriage soon after the project, and this conscious thought projected itself into the subconscious as wish fulfillment and anxiety. This is the only recurring symbolism that appears in his nightly experiences.

8-12-50 "Felt the urge to visit my fiancee, but remembered some unfinished work to do, so I changed my mind . . . "

8-15-50 "Walked by the home of my fiancee, but she wasn't home . . . "

8-17-50 "Felt the presence of fiancee, but could not see her anywhere about me . . . "

During this first week E appears to have had a superconscious dream. The emotion and clarity of the subject matter does create the impression of superconscious origin.

8-16-50 "C and a group were going to meet the Master. When we met Him, His eyes were not open. We sat around a table on the terrace, and C asked questions about astrology. C received kind and helpful answers. It was a nice serene atmosphere, but I was a little frightened on first meeting the Christ . . . "

F's Dream Experiences

Physical: o. Subconscious: 2. Superconscious: o.

F recorded only two dreams for the entire week. Of these two, one seems to be wish fulfillment, and the other remains unclassified; though it too appears under the subconscious heading. As an example, we note:

8-17-50 "Rushed to H.L. and said, "Something astounding has happened with the ESP cards. I can reach very high scores in clairvoyance, but my telepathy remains just about the same . . . ' "

Upon examination of the ESP scoring, nothing extraordinary

could be found in clairvoyance which would motivate a wish-fulfillment dream.

G's Dream Experiences

Physical: 4. Subconscious: 5. Superconscious: 0.

G is the kind of young man who seems to enjoy foods of various types. The four physical dreams pertained to satisfying his stomach — from liver and onions, to jelly sandwiches and peanut butter. The reader will recall that specific diets were followed throughout the entire project, thus creating restrictions upon individual tastes. Therefore, if an individual liked foods of all types, he would naturally satisfy this urge in dream manifestations when thwarted in his desires.

G has several symbols that recur and when they appear, the dream contents are quite similar. Three times during the first week he dreams of being in the library, either doing work or meeting someone. This symbology could mean a point where friends meet, or, by speculation, it could mean that the mind of this individual is anxious for further knowledge. As examples, we find the following entries:

8-13-50 "Found myself outside of the library getting into a battle of wits with Groucho Marx . . . "

8-14-50 "Went to the library to do some research work . . . "

8-16-50 "Had forgotten a date with the girls and found myself rushing toward the library to possibly meet them there . . . "

Summary of First Week's Dreams

Entering then upon a review of the first week's activities during the unconscious state called sleep, we find that the dreams manifested during this period may be classified under the following headings:

PHYSICAL: 11

    a. Food: 7
    b. Libido: 4
    c. Other causes: 0

SUBCONSCIOUS: 34

    a. Wish Fulfillment: 9
    b. Fears and Anxieties: 7
    c. Solution of Problem: 1
    d. Memories of this life: 6
    e. Self-Examination: 5
    f. Telepathy: 0
    g. Clairvoyance: 1

h. Precognition: 0
i. Memory of Past Lives: 0
j. Unclassified: 5

SUPERCONSCIOUS: 1

a. Spiritual Experience: 1

One interesting point which may be noted here is that five of the seven participants dreamed of the symbol, boat or ship. This symbol manifested in just about the same manner. The symbol may be universal; a going onward, advancing, moving or some other such meaning. From the Cayce records, we find that water has been interpreted as life, or the living way.

Thus during the first week of the project, we have 11 dreams in the physical, 34 within the many areas of the subconscious, and 1 in the spiritual domain of the superconscious.

In the second week, you will remember, the pressure was released; so we should be able to note any spiritual growth that may be taking place. If any such growth is transpiring, we should also be able to note the change through the dream manifestations of the seven participants. So, may we now focus our observations upon the dream adventures of the second week.

Second Week

A's Dream Experiences

Physical: 0. Subconscious: 5. Superconscious: 0.

A appears to have had a dream which we might be able to place in the subconscious realm of activity, but may also be classified as one of past-life experience. The essence of actuality in its content and the emotional components create an atmosphere of a past-incarnation experience. To quote from his journal:

8-18-50 "There is a man who has an important job, in which he uses a map. He explores new sections of the country. He is middle-aged and has a distinguished record. An old friend and companion is his lieutenant; the rest of the crew seem content and happy.

"This middle-aged man settles down at one of the advanced outposts in a section which I think is New York. He gets unreasonably angry at the lieutenant when he receives the signal that the prisoners have escaped. His relationship with the subordinate officer turns toward hate.

"A battle takes place with the escaped prisoners, and in the course of it most of his trusty followers are lost, killed. The lieutenant was then given the command to take the majority of the men and go forth into another section, or region. The captain was discredited for the whole action, and now faced a dim future in comparison to the past. He looked at the map of the new region to which he was going, and knew that the lieutenant was not too far from there; he hoped that things could be patched up again between them . . . "

If we are willing to consider the aspect of an early American incarnation, this dream could fit into the past-life category.

The symbol, policemen, has been dropped from the dream experiences, or has taken on one of the many disguises supplied by the subconscious. In the dreams that transpired during the second week, we can note the same emotional content, like that of the first dream, but being carried out in other circumstances.

8-19-50 "I was playing ball with the fellows and they turned against me. I took refuge in my house from all the players. . . "

8-20-50 "A woman was going to judge the characters of my brother and me. My brother wished to be nice to her, but I had heard about her and decided to stick by my guns and be the opposite . . . "

The reader will note the similarity in personality patterns of A and that of the captain. Is it possible that A is the main character in the first dream, even though he does not identify himself directly?

The conscious effort by this young man to create positive personality patterns has caused a conflict. A appears to be still fighting hate, fear, and anger. This is an excellent example of what the records and orthodox psychology speak of so often — conflict of forces within the individual — the waging of war between the forces of good and evil.

There is one other dream which must be brought to the attention of the reader. I think we find here our first evidence of a telepathic communication while in the sleeping state.

8-23-50 "My friend and I met two good-looking girls on board ship. We got to know them and later met them in Virginia Beach . . . "

Let us compare this with the dream had by B on the very same night!

B's Dream Experiences

Physical: 1. Subconscious: 1. Superconscious: 0.

B records a dream which he terms a memory of a high-school-senior cruise. From his journal we note the following entry:

8-23-50 "This dream has to do with a boat trip across a lake. The people I remember are: another fellow, two girls, a cab driver, and myself. First I find myself with the others, in a cab driving toward the docking area; it appears to be a resort type of trip.

79

Nothing significant seems to happen. It is much like the three-day senior cruise . . . "

A and B dream of the same type of experience, though one is more detailed than the other. The identical manifestation is either just coincidence or may be one of true telepathic exchange. The ultimate conclusion is for the reader to decide.

C's Dream Experiences

Physical: 4. Subconscious: 6. Superconscious: 2.

C appears to be under a certain amount of pressure now, as to the restrictions in diet. The four physical dreams have to do with foods of various types. This pressure was not evident during the previous week but manifests quite strongly during the second. Note the journal entries:

8-18-50 "Was in school listening to a lecture on foods. The speaker stated that we don't need to eat . . . "

8-18-50 "Went down town with a friend of mind, and he purchased a box of Ritz crackers . . . "

8-19-50 "A group of friends and I were going to see a movie called the 'Passover,' but I was quite undecided whether to go . . . "

8-21-50 "Was talking to a girl friend of mine. She was having trouble with eating problems. I stated that she should eat vegetables of different kinds and not just any old junk . . . "

8-24-50 "Was with a group that were swimming. After awhile, they brought out a round tray with pork sausages and pancakes. I knew that the pancakes would be o.k., but that I shouldn't eat the sausages because of the project. . . "

It is very interesting to note how the subconscious keeps on working with the problems that we meet in waking life. C appears to be trying very hard to overcome temptation and what he now thinks are bad eating habits.

The recurring symbol which made itself known in the first week is still quite active: that of washing dishes. C is still going through what appears to be self-examination.

8-19-50 'Was in the kitchen helping mother wash the supper dishes. . . "

8-21-50 "Found myself in the A.R.E. kitchen, washing dirty dishes after the meal. There was much material on them which had to be soaked off . . . "

For the first time since the beginning of the project, C appears to have superconscious dreams — a manifestation of spiritual purposes and ideals because of accent upon such development. From his notebook, we find the following notations:

8-20-50 "Dreamed of being spoken to about the seven glands and was told that if I wanted to be one with The Christ, the glands would have to be purified. . ."

8-21-50 "Told those about me that there was no sense in shooting me, because 1 would reincarnate again anyway. Then I ducked into a clothes closet to escape. There, in the closet, I was counselled and told that 1 could escape anything through Christ's power and why didn't 1 do so, now. I think I did. Then I saw people as lights being attracted to Christ. Some were so bright that I could not separate them; the others were so small that they could scarcely be seen. . ."

Because of the tenacity of the washing-dishes symbology, the author wonders whether this may not represent the purification of the glands which C dreams of in his spiritual experience. Washing dishes may well represent the cleansing of the glands. This statement naturally is speculative, but the undertones in C's dreams could rightly create such an impression.

D's Dream Experiences

Physical: 2. Subconscious: 4. Superconscious: 0.

Two of the six dreams recorded by D were physical, and pertained to foods.

8-19-50 "Under my arm I had a package in which were fried eggs. . ."

8-22-50 "I was sitting upon a jutting point from a mast. While sitting there, I was eating from a can, scooping it out with a spoon; it appeared to be meat of some kind. . ."

In the journal of this young man, we find our only verified dream of precognition. To quote from his notebook:

8-24-50 "A friend of my sister brought an apparatus to our house that has a motor on a base of some sort. This mechanism does flip-flops around the room when the cord is plugged into the electrical circuit. . ."

When D went home after the project, he found that his sister had a mechanical horse, which we are familiar with as being used for exercising; therefore, the dream experience of two weeks previous is verified.

E's Dream Experience

Physical: 3. Subconscious: 4. Superconscious: 3.

In the dreams of E we still find the recurring symbol or literal image of his prospective wife. Since the dream content is just about the same as transcribed in the previous week, we will not need to give examples of his notations.

One very interesting point that emerges in E's dreams is the ever greater intensity of self-examination which appears and carries on into the superconscious. Note these three dreams that appear to be introspective and spiritual in essence.

8-20-50 "C was explaining a wonderful experience of how he saw the image of Christ. He said that our preparation thus far seems inadequate in order to have an experience as C had. I then gained an impression of the need for individual preparation as the primary goal, not just talking about certain areas. . . "

The reader will remember that C had a similar experience on the same date. C may have passed the experience over to E by telepathic impression. In all fairness to the boys involved, I think we could classify the identical experience as similar in the realm of the superconscious. Go back to the dream by C on 8-20-50 and compare the parallelism and continuation of the entire dream.

To continue in the same frame of reference:

8-22-50 "Dreamed that I was having a direct communication with a higher source. I was told that I need more gentleness and patience with self, others, and especially with fiancee . . . "

In this last selection, we find an excellent example of the philosophizing trend of the subconscious, working in conjunction with the spiritual values found in the superconscious. This dream is not only self-examination, but also seems to be a direct message from his higher source itself.

8-24-50 "Am seeing elements in self as forms: criticism and selfishness. They are trying to weigh the balance. I became aware that I must pray more — must create longer quiet periods. Patience is my greatest need. Then I cry out, 'What can I do that may be helpful?' Right after this I heard music, which seemed to herald the approach of opening the seven seals. I knew He was near by. I could not fully appreciate the quality and tone of the music, which may have been caused by the debris in the subconscious not yet cleared out. The whole dream gradually faded and I awoke. . . "

F's Dream Experiences

Physical: 1. Subconscious: 2. Superconscious: 0.

This participant has the first clear and concise dream which we may be able to attribute to a physical source other than libido or food. F dreams of hearing the sound of rushing water, that's all. The most logical explanation is that he was staying in a house which is not too far from the ocean; he heard the sound of the sea while in the sleeping state:

The other two experiences recorded by F appear to be of selfexamination, yet have the undertones of fear and anxiety — fear of being a failure in life or vocation.

82

Physical: 3. Subconscious: 7. Superconscious: 0.

G appears to have changed his attitude toward foods, for only one dream contains this item — again it is peanut butter sandwiches! These physical dreams come into view during the fasting periods and may still act as pacifying agents for former urges.

In the journal of G we detect what looks like another flash-back into a past incarnation. To quote directly from his notebook:

8-19-50 "I was constantly counting bead money that was secured together by heavy leather buttons on each end of the string. Each piece of money had a hole in the center and was attached to the cord, thus making a chain-like affair. There were green colored ones and yellow buttons; the rest were shades I don't remember. I knew what the value of each was, but can't judge or compare as it would be today; it does seem that the green ones were like ten dollars, the yellow ones as five. There I was talking to a man about the bead money. I knew, or felt as though I was in China and could see it was quite hilly. The houses or other surroundings I can't remember. . . "

Summary of Second Week's Dreams

We observe in this second week that the pattern has changed somewhat from that of the first week, though in many cases it still remains a constant.

PHYSICAL: 14

    a. Libido: 5
    b. Foods: 7
    c. Other Causes: 2

SUBCONSCIOUS: 29

    a. Wish Fulfillment: 3
    b. Fears and Anxieties: 5
    c. Solution of Problem: 0
    d. Memories of this life: 5
    e. Self-examination: 7
    f. Telepathy: 2
    g. Clairvoyance: 0
    h. Precognition: 1
    i. Memory of Past Life: 2
    j. Unclassified: 4

SUPERCONSCIOUS: 5

    a. Spiritual Experience: 5

Again we note that the same symbol repeats in the dreams of these young men, though at times to a greater or lesser degree. In other cases it has altogether changed as the participant focused his mind upon higher ideals. The symbol of boat or ship is still being manifested in the dreams – this time by four of the seven participants.

Let us go into the third week, and then we will be able to draw a weekly comparison of the entire experiment.

Third Week

A's Dream Experiences

Physical: 2. Subconscious: 9. Superconscious: 0.

We can still note the same pattern which A has been following throughout the entire project.

8-27-50 "I had a dream in which I had two guns and was blazing away..."

8-28-50 "I took off from my home because the land was doomed. On the way out I had to fight off Indians. I had my dog with me but the job was to get by the Indian defenses..."

8-28-50 "I was part of a gang of gentlemen thieves..."

Yes, it is true that many of the negative patterns still crop up in A's dreams, but more and more positive experiences are beginning to come through. Dreams of violence are slowly giving way to self-examination on the positive level. Note the following entries in the third week:

8-28-50 "Was talking to two men about literature. My book on Browning was overdue at the library, but I wasn't worried about the fine, so I gave the fellow the book. I went home but invited him to a study group meeting. I felt that the spiritual ideals and meditation would do him some good. He said that we could help each other..."

8-31-50 "My fraternity brothers reprimanded me for ignoring them for so long a time. I then made peace with them and again took up my place with them..."

8-31-50 "H.L. told me that I had just missed the open door by a hair's breadth last night. It would have been successful if I had known how to use the blank-out period to advantage..."

A has had a long hard struggle with negative conditions within himself, but I think he has reached the point where they will begin to dissipate. Do you agree?

B's Dream Experiences

Physical: 1. Subconscious: 5. Superconscious: 1.

B, in the third week, begins to record his nightly experiences in detail. By observing selections from his notebook, several aspects make themselves known. His dreams appear to be a combination of wish-fulfillment, self-examination, and ideology of the superconscious. To quote:

8-27-50 "I was in a room with twelve people. I was asked to read from the Bible but my vision kept blurring. I then passed the Bible to another on my right. I remember the person to whom I gave it was surprised, and flushed because he wasn't used to reading in a group. . ."

8-28-50 "Most of this dream involved my helping a girl of my age. She had led a bad life and was now suffering for it. I kept on talking to this girl to lift her from the cycle of circumstances in which she now found herself. . ."

8-29-50 "I was talking to my minister about my giving the sermon today, for I had a lot that I wanted to say. I came out onto the preaching platform in the preacher's large robe which was much too big for me. People laughed at me, but I kept right on talking. . ."

8-30-50 "This dream was something about my job as youth director in the church. The man who had had the job before me wanted it back. This man's daughter came by, and the friend who was with me said I could easily say something that would be mean or resentful. I told him it wouldn't be right and I refused. . ."

The reader will note the pattern whcih B seems to be following. It is regrettable that we did not have enough data from the first and second week, so that a comparison could be made.

[B's journal is an excellent example of what can happen if one will only take the time to record his dreams. First there were none, then just a dribble, and now a flowing stream.]

C's Dream Experiences

Physical: 2. Subconscious: 11. Superconscious: 2.

The recurring symbol of washing dishes, which C has had for the first two weeks, now has disappeared entirely from his dreams. It appears to have been replaced by colors, which is the most predominant factor in the third week. Of the fourteen dreams that C records, 10 of them have colors. This was not especially noted before.

8-26-50 "I was walking up a rocky pathway and saw some beautiful rocks with fossils on them. They were quite shiny in tones, mostly greens and blues, also some pinks and violets. I took a sample of each and started down the mountain. . ."

8-30-50 "I was looking at some neckties. I saw many different colors, most of which were green, blue, and yellow. . ."

C has a dream which appears to be self-examination and philosophical in content:

8-25-50 "Got into a boat and traveled around the base of a mountain. By putting out the anchor and pulling the boat by the anchor chain, it would move forward. . . "

C interprets his own dream as follows: "The anchor seemed to mean this: 'We have an anchor that keeps the soul steadfast and sure, while the billows roll.' "

And as the last selection from C's journal, we find evidence of superconscious manifestations.

8-27-50 "Was walking with another fellow and girl. Suddenly we saw a pink and green spark winding in circles near us. 'The Holy Spirit,' we cried. It came upon us and circled around, crackling as it went. We were highly elated and began to go onward. This was a very real experience. . . "

8-30-50 "I was with a healer and saw him perform upon a malformed Atlantean, a man with head and body as a man, but feet and hands like a horse. We saw the Master coming in an oddly-shaped boat. We then rushed into our boat and began to paddle toward Him. . . "

As the project progressed C went through various stages that were quite evident. First the cleansing process that made itself known through the washing of dishes. Then the trouble with foods, and the correction of this attitude. Now he appears to have most of his dreams in color that are either philosophical or spiritual in content. Here is an excellent example of step-by-step growth, or at least the evidence points in that direction.

D's Dream Experiences

Physical: 3. Subconscious: 3. Superconscious: 0.

Of the three physical dreams that D had in the third week, two pertain to foods, especially liver steaks.

8-30-50 "Liver steaks were being cooked by Nelson Eddy, and he was peppering them. I yelled to him not to pepper mine. . . "

The only dream which the author has been able to uncover which has a spiritual essence is one had by D on the last day of the project.

8-31-50 "There was a meditation meal in progress; I was a little late, though I did feel I was on time. They were seated in a rough circle in nature's surroundings. I joined them. . . "

It is almost impossible to draw any kind of tentative conclusion concerning the dreams of D, because we have had very little material to work with. It is up to the reader to determine whether there is any evidence of growth or change in personality patterns. D did not record any dreams in the first week, except several of libido activity. He then seemed to go into foods during the second week; the final week's dreams remain largely unclassified.

E's Dream Experiences

Physical: 0. Subconscious: 6. Superconscious: 1.

E records a dream concerning another participant, that of B, and his changing attitude. To quote:

8-25-50 "Dreamed of B. He was walking into the house after having an interview with H.L. Have the impression that all doubts and incorrect thinking are being cleared through dreams. . . "

The reader will recall that B had recorded 7 dreams in this third week — more than the total of the other two weeks. B's dreams did take an introspective turn. Therefore E may be right in drawing such a subconscious conclusion. Is he right?

E is one of the participants who kept on dreaming about ships throughout the project. The following entry may give us an answer as to what the ship represented.

8-30-50 "Seemed to be on board ship and was preparing to leave. I remember looking into the mirror before I left. Some of the other boys were with me, and we all seemed to be getting ready to leave together. . . "

The symbol of a ship may be a representation of the project itself. Now that the three-weeks journey is coming to a close, they are getting ready to leave this vessel which has been their home for the three-week period. True, it may be reading much into a simple dream, but it is very logical that the project itself be represented as a ship by the subconscious, with the director as the navigator.

In the last selection from E's notebook we find an experience that is much like that of C, even though they occur on different days. To quote directly from his journal:

8-31-50 "Was standing near the beach with some of the other boys. We all saw a beautiful light in the sky, in the East, over the water. It was beautiful in color — white, blue, light green, and pink that faded into a sparkling lavender and violet. We all knew that the Creator was near by, for we could feel His presence. . . "

Note the similarity of this experience and the one C had on 8-27-50. It is quite odd that they begin to dream of lights and color in the final week, is it not?

There is no need to summarize E's dreams, for they are quite clear and show definite change in content. Here again, subconscious change makes itself known through the dream manifestations of the individual.

F's Dream Experiences

Physical: 1. Subconscious: 2. Superconscious: 1.

In this young man's notebook, there are two clear examples of growth — one is subconscious in essence and the other philosophical and spiritual in origin.

8-26-50 "I dreamed that everyone was offered a choice — either learning of the pituitary gland here or spending a lifetime, perhaps in suffering, learning about the pituitary elsewhere."

The pituitary gland has often been mentioned in the Edgar Cayce records as being the highest spiritual gland in the human body.

8-30-50 "I dreamed vividly that my brother came over to me and was explaining why I didn't go to God during the night. He said that I had too much sand in my hair, and I asked him whether he meant figuratively or literally — he said literally; my hair needed a good washing and then I would be ready to meet Him. . . "

This experience is self-explanatory, yet there appears to be a higher self informing him of his lack of preparation to meet God. It would have been interesting to note the dreams on the following night, but the project was completed. Do you think any change has taken place within this young man over the three-week period? Observe his dreams.

G's Dream Experiences

Physical: 1. Subconscious: 5. Superconscious: 0.

8-25-50 "I heard or thought I heard the voice of Edgar Cayce, and he was telling me a story. I don't remember it in detail, but it seems to have been something about a decision. I had a choice of seven decisions or seven glands. He then went on about making the decision to serve. . . "

This dream will remain unclassified. Whether it was a direct communication, or just the subconscious using one of its many disguises, is for the reader to decide. It has been entered because each member has dreamed, at one time or another, about the glands.

In the final dream we find a clairvoyant experience that has been verified. To quote from his journal:

8-30-50 "I was searching through Mr. Cayce's office looking for some books on numerology and astrology, and I then came across a red-covered book that looked like an encyclopedia. In the book were pictures of models used in anatomy studies; I immediately put the book back and left the office. . . "

There is a book of this description in the study, but not within sight of anyone coming into the office. The book is one published by a midwestern art institute for anatomy studies, involving bone and muscle structure, also the drawing of skin texture. Thus we see that G did have a clairvoyant dream, for he described the book and its content, even though he was not consciously aware of its presence in the study.

In the first week we found G revolving around the recurring symbolism of library and feeding himself every night in his dreams. The second week showed that these recurring symbols had either disappeared or escaped detection by taking up another disguise.

The final week's experiences involve clairvoyance and one of self-examination, plus several other introspective experiences. Has this participant changed since the first week?

Compiling now the results of the third and final week of the experiment, we find the following tabulation of the speculative observations.

PHYSICAL: 10

    a. Libido: 7
    b. Foods: 2
    c. Other causes: 1

SUBCONSCIOUS: 42

    a. Wish Fulfillment: 6
    b. Solution of Problem: 1
    c. Fears and Anxieties: 7
    d. Memories of this Life: 6
    e. Self Examination: 12
    f. Telepathy: 0
    g. Clairvoyance: 0
    h. Precognition: 2
    i. Memory of past Life: 2
    j. Unclassified: 6

SUPERCONSCIOUS: 5

    a. Spiritual Experience: 5

Summary of Seven Sets of Data

In drawing up a summary of the entire project, may we first show the weekly comparative survey of the seven college-age participants. This entails the total number of dreams and their general classification.

		Physical	Subconscious	Superconscious
A	First Week:	0	8	0
	Second Week:	0	5	0
	Third Week:	2	9	0
B	First Week:	0	0	0
	Second Week:	1	1	0
	Third Week:	1	5	1
C	First Week:	2	14	0
	Second Week:	4	6	2
	Third Week:	2	11	2
D	First Week:	3	0	0
	Second Week:	2	4	0
	Third Week:	3	3	0
E	First Week:	2	5	1
	Second Week:	3	4	3
	Third Week:	0	6	1
F	First Week:	0	2	0
	Second Week:	1	2	0
	Third Week:	1	2	1
G	First Week:	4	5	0
	Second Week:	3	7	0
	Third Week:	1	5	0
		35	104	11

Progress Map

The following chart is a progress map of the changes in dream experiences that took place as the experiment matured.

PHYSICAL: 35	1st Week	2nd Week	3rd Week
a. Libido	4	5	7
b. Foods	7	7	2
c. Other Causes	0	2	1
SUBCONSCIOUS: 104			
a. Wish Fulfillment	9	2	6
b. Fears and Anxieties	7	5	7
c. Solution of Problem	1	0	1
d. Memories of this Life	6	5	6
e. Self Examination	5	7	12
f. Telepathy	0	2	0
g. Clairvoyance	1	0	2
h. Precognition	0	1	0
i. Memory of Past Lives	0	2	2
j. Unclassified	5	4	6
SUPERCONSCIOUS: 11			
a. Spiritual Experience	1	5	5
	46	47	57

Total number of dreams according to participant:

(A) 24
(B) 9
(C) 43
(D) 15
(E) 25
(F) 9
(G) 25

The above shows that 150 dreams were used in formulating this comparative study.

General Summary

The die is cast. The hypotheses have been placed beside the laboratory evidence. Now let us gather all the information that we have accumulated from several sources. Whether your opinion be pro or con: on one side we have man, the organism; on the other, man, the possessor of a soul.

In respect to sleep, science states:

1. Sleep is the normal periodic loss of consciousness of a special nature, and is characteristic of many animals.
2. Lack of stimulation to the sensory data plus a form of fatigue appear to be conducive to that unconscious state called sleep.
3. In sleep the body temperature and metabolism rate become lower; heartbeat, respiration, and circulation slow down somewhat;
4. At present physical science is unable to state why sleep is necessary, other than it is indispensable to continuation of life.

The Edgar Cayce records state:

. . . little of this can be called a true analysis of what happens to the body either physical, mental, subconscious or spiritual, when it loses itself in such repose.   5754-1

Sleep is a shadow of that intermission of the earth's experiences, that state called death.   5754-1

The organs which form a part of that portion known as the inactive, or not necessary for conscious movement, keep right on functioning. The heartbeat, pulsations, the assimilating and excretory system keep right on functioning; yet there are periods during such a rest when even the heart, the circulation, may be said to be at rest.   5754-1

Sleep is that period when the soul takes stock of what it has acted upon during one rest period to another, making or drawing — as it were — comparisons that make life itself in its essence.   5754-2

In respect to dreams, science states:

1. Freud approaches dreams basically from the standpoint of repressed desires, or forbidden sex impulses. Present conflicts and frustrations are of the libido in origin.
2. Jung rejects Freud's concept, and looks upon dreams as an expression of the "collective unconscious" and the desire of man to be a creator in his own right.
3. Adler believes that dreams are the expression of desire for power and security.
4. The psychologist places little value upon dreams, other than

that they are devised to keep the sleeper in that state. They acknowledge the psycho-somatic dreams, the internal or external stimuli, and even agree upon dreams of anxiety, the mental conflicts. But the rest, or the majority, are merely automatic and chance play of the cerebral associational mechanisms.

The Edgar Cayce readings state:

As we have given, many receive such impressions and might be benefited physically, mentally and spiritually, by following or adhering to the many lessons that are given through such impressions.   900-13

As in dreams, these forces of the subconscious, when taken or correlated into those forms that relate to the various phases of the individual, give that individual a better understanding of self, when correctly interpreted, or when correctly answered.   3744-4, A-41

All visions and dreams are given for the benefit of the individual, if he would but interpret them correctly.   294-15

[Dreams] are the reflection of (1) physical conditons, with variations of same; (2) the subconscious, with conditions relating to the physical body and its actions, either through the mind or through the elements of the spiritual entity; (3) a projection from the spiritual forces to the subconscious of the individual.
                    294-15

Conclusion

The writer has assumed that man is an organism possessed of a soul. This view obviously involves the hypothesis that we are living in two worlds at the same time: the material plane in which man is intended to act; and also the cosmic life in that spiritual plane, which is the native environment of the soul.

The waking personality is adapted to the needs of earthly life. The personality of sleep maintains the fundamental connection between the organism and the spiritual world. This other self-within-self supplies the body with spiritual energy during sleep and also develops itself by exercising its own spiritual faculties, based on what it has done in the past.

As you consider this material for signposts for your own search, keep in mind the value which dreams may hold for you. Within is a friend who stands by to guide and help as we travel forward, ever forward. This is a friend to whom all our troubles appear to go, without need of the spoken word. The spiritual you stands fast to aid in solving a problem, to forewarn you of events and to give you insight into the behavior of the waking you.

Begin now to record your dreams. Be persistent; be consistent.

Learn the picture language of the subconscious. Discover the hidden meaning behind the disguises of recurring symbols.

Here is high adventure within, not without; and as we continue on this ever-flowing stream, may we some day learn to be a sparkle in the eye of God, not a grain of sand.